Kept Promises

PROSPERING IN A PANDEMIC

Stories Compiled by

ALANDRIA LLOYD

THE Writer's
BLOCK

Contents

Prelude

THE NOVEL CORONA VIRUS or COVID-19 and its deadly effects will be echoed throughout history for decades to come. There will be many history books written to detail the events that took place during 2020. Our grandchildren, great-grandchildren, and family members for generations to come hear about the great Corona Virus.

The pandemic took everyone by surprise, and no one knew what to expect. There were many low moments and losses that occurred, but there were also gains. Many people prospered like never before and accomplished lifelong dreams. So, while historians, journalists, and the media will always speak about the tragedies that occurred, the writers of "Kept Promises" wanted to shed light and share how many people prospered during a time when everyone expected to see a decline.

Covid hit the world hard, but the provisions of God hit even harder. The authors of this soon-to-be history book hope that the readers will be encouraged to know that our Father in Heaven will always protect and provide no matter what happens on the earth. The stories within the pages of this anthology promise to uplift low spirits, encourage wounded hearts and soothe worried minds. So grab a cup of coffee, snuggle up in your favorite chair, and allow this book to be the inspiration you need to overcome any trial that may try to overtake you.

1

You Can't Get There Unless God Takes You There

IT HAS BEEN MORE THAN 100 years since the last pandemic, which I did not personally experience. However, when one hit this time around, I can tell you that there were individuals who lost their jobs, homes, and the most devastating, their lives. So, during a time of lack for so many, it seems illogical to talk about prosperity. But that is what I am going to share. Not only did my family thrive, but we lived in the overflow. Make no mistake about it, that overflow was God's grace and mercy.

There comes a time when the promises God has revealed to you in private begin to unfold in public. The thing about a promise is that it is an assurance that one will do a sure thing or that something will happen. With God, you can always be confident that if He said it, it is settled, and it will come to pass. Hold steadfast, like you did when you were a child, and your parents made a promise to you. You looked for it without hesitation or doubt. That is how we are to hold on to God's promises. Reflecting upon assurances, I think of a song we sing in our church with the chorus of, *"For He promised me if I live right...for He promised me, my battles He would fight, for He promised me that He would take care of me."* I depend on those sentiments every day of my life.

First, I must acknowledge the fact that God kept and sustained everyone in my household, even adding a new little person, and allowed us to maintain employment. This is not to disregard others and their loss; it is simply a statement of pure appreciation. Over the years, there have been many times when I did not know how I would make it; stressed, scared, sickness in my family, not a dime to my name, but God! God delivered every time. (insert dance) This period was different. We had no moments of fear. It was a time of healing, development, and growth, in other words, prosperity.

The first thing I will share in this testimony is the miraculous transformation of my son by way of a stem cell transplant to treat Sickle Cell Disease. When the virus started spreading, our son's initial treatment was complete, but he was far from recovered or safe. The therapy had decimated his entire immune system, so for him to go out into public or to come in contact with someone Covid positive could prove deadly. We traveled back home, by plane, from the treatment location, continued to care for him, and over the past year, he has been well and has never tested positive for Covid. That is only God.

Now, in case you did not know, let me introduce you to the one I serve; He is a God of "but wait, there's more," so not only did He keep our son, but He also allowed me to write the story. My first book, released in December 2020, details the transplant journey for our family. You might think that the blessings stopped there, but oh no, my God is greater and supplies more than what we can imagine. With the book's launch, many doors have opened, and God brought back to my remembrance, the word He spoke to me some years ago. God directed me to advocate for children. I have always had a huge heart for children, and often find myself supporting them in different capacities. However, the level of advocacy to which God would raise me took some trials and tribulations; pain; dead-ends, and finally, victory with my own child's health to push me to stand in the gap for others regarding their care. When you have an assignment directly from God, you might as well get ready to soar.

The phrase 'next level' has taken on a new meaning. Not only am I advocating in a new way, but I am now in a position to help others advocate for their loved ones. Still, that is not how the story ends. It was during the pandemic, God guided and provided for me to start my business. I had been seeking an answer of how to couple His vision for me with a way of provision. It became clear when I followed the instruction to write the book. From there, the opportunities rushed in and continue to present themselves regularly. More writing, entrepreneurship, speaking, features, and the best part of it all, I am doing it all under the direction of the Holy Spirit.

What I have learned in this time of abundance is that I cannot fathom the reach of God. My hopes, dreams, and wishes do not compare to the extent of God's scope. The things we think of are just the beginning. They are motivators that push us toward God and His vision. I am excited about the increase to come, as every round goes higher and higher. We have to listen for direction and move when God says move. Whatever He tells you to do, you must trust that all is for your good. I often hear people saying, trust the process, and what that means is to rely upon the direction your journey is taking. When you trust, you can sleep better at night knowing that where you are going, God is taking you.

There is a scripture found in Jeremiah that speaks profoundly of the plan God has for you. The next time you are in a personal pandemic, remember to trust God's intent, and He will see you through.

"For I know the plans I have for you," declares the Lord, "plans to prosper you and not to harm you, plans to give you hope and a future." Jeremiah 29:11

Patrice Sterling is The Advocate Mom! She is fueled by her faith, family, and calling to advocate for children, specifically those with Sickle Cell Disease. She is an author, writer, and care strategist. She teaches caregivers how to establish a partnership with their provider, unlock their ability to question the experts, and uncover ways to be heard by never giving up. Lastly, but most importantly, in all things, she is a God girl!

2

Christ in the Crisis

WHAT IS A CRISIS? It is a sudden occurrence of pain, distress, or disordered function. I am sure at one point in your life you've experienced a crisis or crises. I can definitely mark the year 2020 as being a crisis. It was filled with the sudden occurrence of pain from so many losing loved ones, to distress from students, teachers, and parents having to adjust to a new way of learning and filled with extreme disorder. Although we have entered a new year, the effects of that year still linger today. Thankfully, I can still say that God is good.

Despite the chaos and confusion in our society, God has blessed me with such peace, even in the midst of a pandemic. Through Jesus and His loving kindness, I was given the opportunity to become a first-time author and business owner. I decided to not allow what was happening in my environment to dictate my outcome. Many times, we miss the blessings of God because we're too focused on what's happening around us instead of what God is trying to do through us. Instead of placing our focus on the things of this world, we should be placing it on the kingdom of God. He will be the source of your strength and will help lead you along your journey. Whether you're facing an emotional crisis or a physical one, He has everything you need to ensure that you overcome it.

I can remember the emotions I felt during the beginning stages of writing my first book, entitled "The Journey to Birthing Your Purpose." During this time, a lot of businesses were closing because of COVID-19, and I had recently been terminated from my job due to this virus. God had impressed upon my heart to write this book, and all I could think about was, where would this money come from for me to complete this task. For three months, I was out of work but was provided the time and money needed to not only fund this entire assignment but was also able to pay on all my bills in a timely manner. Now, I could have looked at my current situation and decided not to write the book. Instead, I trusted that God would not have given me the task without providing me with the resources needed to complete it. Through my obedience, I was able to encourage others as well as release pain and insecurities that I had been harboring for years.

There are many instances in the Bible where obedience played a key role in someone being protected and/or victorious during major crises. Let's start with Noah and the flood. Because Noah was obedient, God was able to provide Noah with the resources needed to build an Ark. This ark protected Noah and his family from a mass flood that wiped out an entire nation (Genesis 7-9). You can also look at the three Hebrew men who were thrown into fire for not following the orders of King Nebuchadnezzar II. These three men by the names of Shadrach, Meshach, and Abednego were thrown into a fire for not bowing to a false god (idol). However, these three men were also protected because they chose to remain faithful to God. These two examples depict how critical it is to give God access to be Lord of your life, not just when you're going through difficult times but in every decision that you make.

When you are connected and committed to God, He will always give you just what you need, whenever you need it. The scripture says in John 15:4, "Abide in me and I in you. As the branch cannot bear fruit of itself, unless it abides in Me." To abide means to remain steadfast or faithful, therefore, as long as we remain faithful to God, He is sure to remain faithful to us. This isn't to say that you only seek God for your own selfish desires, but to seek His face, His character, and to study His word so that you may know how to withstand when trials arrive in your life. If last year taught us anything, it should have been that hindsight is 20/20.... literally. There was so much that was revealed, and so much that occurred during that year that could have easily driven me insane. But because I kept my focus on Christ, I was able to maintain a peace of mind and my health and strength.

As we continue throughout this year, remember to seek Christ in every decision you make. Don't allow what you see on social media, or the news outlets to make you forfeit the promises of God. Be obedient to the voice of God and trust that He will provide. Whether it's comfort that you need because of a grief-stricken event that may have taken place, He can be that. If you're searching for a peace of mind due to stress-related circumstances, His word says that He is the prince of peace (Isaiah 9:6). "No, in all these things we are more than conquerors through him who loved us. For I am convinced that neither death nor life, neither angels nor demons, neither the present nor the future, nor the powers, neither height nor depth, nor anything else in all creation, will be able to separate us from the love of God that is in Christ Jesus our Lord" (Romans 8:37-39, NIV). Decide to make this year the year where you will consistently seek all things concerning God and His kingdom. In doing so, you can, and you will conquer every obstacle that arises in your life.

Brittany Winston is a Summit, MS native. She published her first solo project entitled "The Journey to Birthing Your Purpose" in July of 2020, which is a powerful story of how she overcame addiction and depression through Jesus Christ. She writes to encourage others through the transparent and triumphant testimonials of her life. As she continues to express the goodness and faithfulness of God through her writing, she hopes that with every read, someone will find Christ in their own life journey. Along with her being a skilled writer, she is also a small business owner of The Chosen Collection, LLC. It is a faith-based, e-commerce business that sells custom apparel. To find more information about her solo project and/or custom apparel, visit her website at www.shopchosenclltn/home.com.

3

Friendships Force Us to Face Ourselves

OKAY...OKAY. OKAY! Let's just talk about it, friend. It's a pandemic and the first vision we have of that, is of hundreds of people running around in and out of stores trying to stock up on main household items to ensure they're not met with any droughts if the government decides to shut down and have us on lockdown for the whole year, I'm exaggerating...but...hey! It totally seems possible during the COVID-19 pandemic. But one of the things I don't think anyone took the time to stock up on was ensuring they had the emotional support for what was about to take place. Did many people call their friends first to find out what their thoughts were? Or whether their friends had a plan B if all else were to fail? How about how we would support our friends that had to experience losses in their families, business, or career? I don't know about you, but it can get quite lonely in a house, eating all the snacks in the world with no one to really talk to or discuss all the moving parts with. This is what most of my friends, clients, and mentees expressed during the 2020 Pandemic. So, it's safe to say that we were advised to stock up on all the material things, but no one really said, "stock up on friendship and support."

For many, including myself, this became a forced time of isolation and at some point, it seemed like all we had as a companion was our mirrors. It was truly up to us whether we wanted to face it and look at ourselves, but the depth of the person in us was standing right there, waiting for us to see. Many others have lost friends during this pandemic due to a lack of support that they thought would be there for them in a time of need, whether emotionally, physically, or financially. Where are all my friends? Was the outcry of most of the Facebook statuses and direct messages from people that I would read. I mean, you've maxed out the 5k limit on Facebook and have over 3K followers on Instagram and STILL found yourself being lonely because no one could really grasp what you were going through during the pandemic.

For me, I didn't lose many friends, but the isolation showed me just how much more important it is to have pure friendships. These friendships are to hold you accountable and help motivate you to keep pushing through despite the changes. Although this isn't the story for most, I'm grateful that God kept his promises to sustain my friendships even through what I had to endure at the onset of the pandemic.

Early on in 2020, I realized that I needed more of a push from my friends than ever before. There were some relationships that were weighing me down, career issues stirring up, and just an overall lack of confidence in business. The reality was, I had great friendships, but other areas of my life needed attention. At that point, I really had to face some things about myself that were really hard to swallow. Some pills that I never thought I would have to take from my own friends about what was going on were thrown in my face (by the grace of God). Even with my mistakes and not taking heed to some of the advice from my friends, I was lucky to have their support during and after the fact. When one friend betrayed me through the process of releasing a tragic secret to someone else, I forgave them. I learned that I was stronger than I thought I was. I learned that I could actually face other areas of my life that I had not mastered, through the indirect and sometimes direct honesty from my friends.

After I looked in the mirror when I felt like I couldn't turn to anyone around me due to shame of the mistakes I've made, I was able to actively focus on me more. I learned how to be even more vulnerable in my friendships by telling the truth about what I was going through. This made me a better friend and allowed my friends to support me like never before.

See, sometimes we aren't stocked up on support because we aren't honest about what we are going through for many reasons that could be shame, guilt, confusion, or oppression...but there is a breakthrough of support that comes with vulnerability. During this friendship lesson in the pandemic, I was able to plant two businesses surrounding the topic of friendship and heal while making the most I ever have financially during the pandemic. My mentorship program and apparel line quadrupled the amount of income I made monthly. Now, I actively coach women on breaking these barriers and building real support systems during their times of transition, isolation, and what seems like warfare. This is when you need your friends the most.

You might've gone through a lot of things during this pandemic that you haven't shared fully with the friends around you. Or maybe you haven't been surrounded by the friends that you feel you could trust with your shortcomings; either way, I'm sure it wasn't easy to think and process things alone. Therefore, I have become even more passionate about the friendship movement and creating a space for vulnerability, not just with ourselves, but also with the world; even if it's virtually. It's a blessing to have people around you to hold you accountable for your thoughts and behaviors because, friend, we can get lost in the sauce! So how do you stock up on friendship and support during a pandemic? You become vulnerable by allowing friendships to force you to face yourself! God will keep His promise to surround you with people that are fit to journey with you despite who you lose along the way if you continue to trust Him and the process!

Luke 18:29-30 (MSG) "Yes," said Jesus, "and you won't regret it. No one who has sacrificed home, spouse, brothers and sisters, parents, children—whatever—will lose out. It will all come back multiplied many times over in your lifetime. And then the bonus of eternal life!"

Samantha D. Liberal, formally known as The Friendship Enthusiast, is an advocate for the "new friends" movement. It's her desire to help people journeying to purpose experience the blessings and favor that comes with friendship. She is the founder and CEO of Pure Friendships. Through her ministry, she learned what pure friendship really is and what it takes to maintain it!

Friendships are not easy because you're interacting with different people with different morals, mindsets, and beliefs, but it sure is worth it if it is done the right way. Ordained as a Prophet by God, The Friendship Enthusiast uses her God-given gifts to share her story, hoping to impact the way in which people choose to do friendships! She has spoken on panels at events in collaboration for empowerment. As an author and journalist, she plans to bridge the gap between making friends and keeping them!

4

Be Still to Become

I ALWAYS KNEW I wanted to be a writer. In fact, that's what I planned to do after I graduated college. I started applying to grad schools' creative writing programs with the goal of writing a best-selling fiction book. After receiving several rejection letters, I became discouraged and gave up on my dream of writing. I took those rejection letters as a sign that I was not supposed to be a writer and made other plans for my life. But God had other plans for me.

Since I had given up on writing, I ended up working in education. I knew I wanted more and went on a journey of discovering my purpose. I was in a constant state of confusion for years as I explored different things. Starting and stopping became my norm. What I discovered is that none of these were my passion. I had become involved in several activities, so I didn't have much time to be still. Every time I jumped into something new, it became a distraction that prevented me from hearing the voice of God and caused me to lose my voice as a writer.

By 2019, I had settled into my position in higher education. I was content but did not feel any real purpose connected to my work. One day, a colleague noticed the book I was reading. She told me she had just finished reading the same book, so we began to talk about the author's work. During our conversation, I mentioned that I used to write. I will never forget the look on her face when she said, "Used to write?" She seemed so excited and asked if she could read something I had written. I agreed and later reluctantly sent her a copy of a short story I had written. The next day she came into my office and said, "Girl, why are you sitting on your gift?" She enjoyed the story and wanted to hear more from the main character. I thanked her but did not write anything until a year later.

Around April of 2020, I began to get restless. With everything being shut down due to the pandemic, I had no running group, spin class, or yoga class to occupy my time. A mixture of fear and uncertainty caused me to have trouble sleeping. Every night, after finally dozing off, I would wake up at about four a.m. I would lay still, eyes closed, trying to fall back asleep but couldn't. I kept seeing the words "you have a story to tell." I brushed it off as a dream, but the vision would become clearer in the coming days.

One early morning, instead of trying to fall back asleep, I grabbed my phone and started scrolling through Facebook. I came across an ad for a masterclass on writing your story. I watched the ad, and before I knew it, I had clicked on the link to sign up. The next day, I got a call from my dad checking on me. He asked when I was going to write my book and said he had a dream that I would be a best-selling author. I know Facebook "stalks" you with ads related to your viewing and search preferences, but it couldn't have possibly reached my dad. I laughed and told him I was thinking about it. When I said I was thinking about it, that was not true. It was just a lie to get my dad off the phone that eventually became true.

Now that my days were no longer filled with outside activities, I had no choice but to be still. Once I got still, I was finally able to clearly hear from God. At first, when I saw the words "you have a story to tell," I didn't believe that was from God. I didn't think God spoke to me because I didn't audibly hear anything. One evening, I attended a training where the speaker discussed the different ways in which God speaks to us, one of which is by visions. I now understood that God was showing me these words, which I would continue to see until I moved on them. At first, I fought it because I didn't think I had anything to say worth reading. I thought, God, nobody wants to hear my story. So many people have had the same thing happen to them. The more I spoke words of negativity, the more I saw God saying things to me, like "tell your story" or "just write."

I was afraid that no one would want to read my work or that I would be laughed at and talked about. But God had plans for me, and once I yielded to the call, I rediscovered my love for writing. I joined a writing boot camp where I was able to complete my first manuscript in a short time. It wasn't perfect, but I made progress. I found my niche as a writer and began to see purpose behind my words. Once I began to write again, I discovered my voice. We all have a story to tell, and no matter how many others have had a similar experience, your story is unique. Don't let fear, insecurity, or opinions stop you from telling your story. Your words will touch those who were meant to hear what you have to say.

In 2020, I found myself as a writer, discovered purpose in my writing, and got closer to the God in me, as I was no longer blocking out His voice. During the pandemic, God made it so that I had to be still, so I could hear from Him. 1 Samuel 12:16 (NIV) "Now then stand still and see this great thing that the Lord will do before your eyes!" Sometimes we need to stop everything and put our focus on God because if we are not still, God can make it so that we have no choice but to be still.

Monique LaTrice is a new author and higher education professional. She earned a B.A. in English Literature, an M.A. in Communications and is working toward a doctorate. Monique successfully completed an 18-week spiritual leadership and biblical training and is an ordained minister.

Monique's writing projects include the devotional *8 Week Journey of Self Discovery* published in 2018, *Pieces of Me*, a compact biography completed in 2020, and *Late Discovery: How A Half-Adoptee Became Whole*, coming in 2021. She is also a contributing author of Beyond the Book Media's anthology *Speak Up...We Deserve to Be Heard* published in 2021. Monique is an avid reader who enjoys traveling, serving on mission trips, and spinning classes.

As a mother and "Lola," Monique is a beacon of hope for her family and to those whom she is assigned. She is determined to let her light shine. You may find Monique on Facebook.com/authormoniquelatrice and Instagram @dr.moniquelatrice.

5

Strength

Isaiah 40: 29-31 says it best

God gives us strength and increases power of the weak. Everyone gets tired and weary and stumble and fall, but they that put their trust in God, he will give you the STRENGTH you need....

HELLO, 2020!

Well, the year started off okay. A few issues, but it is the New Year, right, so it will get better, right? Ummmm...well, I had thought that things would change for the better. I chose the word 'Strength' for my focus word for 2020. What I mean by my focus word is a group of ladies from my church and text ministry chose a word each year to focus on. Major things happen when you focus on a word that you struggle with. I have participated in this for several years. It has proven to be a great way to stay motivated throughout the year.

Well, business as usual for February. Oh yeah, I was fasting as I usually did on New Years'. My personal fasting started on January 1 to Easter. Yes, a long time, right! I was fasting for direction. So let us fast forward to March when the world shut down. While everyone was home, I still worked maybe eight to ten hours a day for five days, sometimes six. I had no days off due to the virus. Our business picked up. Along with worrying about getting the virus, I had to deal with crazy people. But I survived.

Moving forward.

April is here! One of my favorite months. My birthday is at the end of April. Yes, a Taurus. I was turning 45. I normally do something nice for myself, BUT! This year, things were different. About a week before my birthday, I began to re-evaluate my life. This is where Queen V began, and I started to make some changes in my life. I decided that when my baby girl graduated, then I would only work in ministry. You see, I was ordained as an Evangelist back in 2017.

Well, I worked a lot within my church; I even did Prison Ministry, which was on hold due to the pandemic. I also participated in a bi-weekly Bible study with the elderly. Most of the things I was doing surrounding ministry were placed on hold due to the virus, along with me losing some of my elderly customers from my cleaning business due to the pandemic. I love cleaning for the elderly, as it offers them companionship as well as a clean house. Working within ministry full-time was something I wanted to do for some time now, but the timing was never right. Coupled with timing, I had a daughter who finally found something she was interested in and had a lot of events she was taking part in for the last two years. That was a blessing for my daughter, but Momma's desires had to wait a little longer. Honestly, my daughter was the one who showed real strength this year.

The pandemic canceled her senior year. Her senior year was ruined. She missed her prom, graduation, and a few special projects that she worked so hard for. You see, this young lady was not happy about anything or motivated about anything until she took a culinary class. Senior year is usually a special year. This year, she worked hard on several projects. She had prepared for an extra special competition. This competition was to be held in New Orleans the same week the state shut down. So, this was the beginning of canceled events for her. She also missed the opportunity to pitch her business idea to a class she was attending every

Tuesday and worked very hard in. You see, baby girl had a very busy schedule, and she was very active. The virus has taken away many of her opportunities.

With everything shutting down, baby girl began to lose focus. There was nothing to do and nowhere to go. So, she mustered up a little strength and began to apply for jobs, and she got her first paying job. The pay didn't matter, she just wanted something to do. Fast food here she comes. She took her job very seriously, but she stayed too long. You see, sometimes you have to find your strength to walk away. Well, baby girl showed her strength within this situation where she never would throw in the towel. Working in fast food industry should be a stepping-stone. She did not want to leave because she felt that she could not do anything else. Usually that's how we get stuck in life's situations. We feel that we can't do anything about the situation or do better than the present situation. This is simply untrue. God will better any situation and help you learn from all your disap-pointments. Fast forward, she has a better-paying job and fewer headaches. See, when you find your strength, any-thing can happen.

So back to me...

Everything I did in 2020 took strength. I ended things I thought I could not live without. I started things I thought I could not do in my life. Most of all, I found my inner strength. I know if no man on this earth has me, my God has my back, and He will guide me into the very reason I was created. Just a few years ago, I learned a big part of my purpose, which is to be a helper/servant. This purpose will take great strength because God's children are selfish, and to be a true servant, you have to serve from your heart and not your inner self. When serving, you must remove self, and that requires great strength.

A scripture I will hold to is Proverbs 31:25, and it says,

"Clothed in Strength and Dignity and I will laugh without fear of my future..."

Velma Albert was born and raised in Louisiana, where she currently resides. Velma is a woman of God; she gave her life to Christ over 18 years ago. Evangelist Albert discovered part of her purpose in life which is to be a helper/servant. Evangelist Velma's plan for the future is to move forward in her newest business adventure, Queen V Coaching and Consulting, where she will be able to help God's people and working in ministry full-time.

She has a simple plan, and with God's help, she will put some things into place real soon. Specializing with the undesirable and the looked over women. Evangelist Albert is currently in Ministry School, she hopes to offer Christian Counseling upon completing and receiving her degree.

A scripture she tries to live by is:

"And whatsoever ye do, do it heartily, as to the Lord, and not unto men" – Colossians 3:23.

6

Pain into Profit

I KNEW THIS YEAR WAS going to be different when Kobe Bryant and his precious daughter died in January. For some reason, their deaths set the tone for the year. But nothing prepared me for this loss that would hit my family. Friday, March 13th, the world was shutting down, country by country, state by state, city by city, as an unknown virus was starting to spread like wildfire. I remember getting up early that day to go to my grandmother's nursing home to hug her and explain to her why we wouldn't be there to visit her for a while. I got there at 8 am and they had already shut her residence down. I stood in the hallway and just cried. I prayed in that moment that God protect her and let us be able to visit her again.

In May, we were finally able to see her through the glass door on her birthday, which made things a lot better for us because, between the months of March and May, I could feel the depression start to settle in me because I was missing my grandmother. My grandmother and I were extremely close, and she moved from Buffalo to Texas, to Georgia with me. Fast forward to August 7th, the nursing home suggested that my mother come in from Buffalo, NY and that we come see her just in case something were to happen to her, and we were unable to see her. I found that to be strange, as they had shut the place down, no one in and no one out. When we went into her room, she was alert, but I could tell that she was dying and held on to see us. The next day, August 8th, I lost a very big piece of me. My heart was and still is broken, as she was my everything.

One thing about my grandmother, she would never want me to curl up under a rock and mourn her. She knew that I was a goal-getter and whatever I put my mind to, I would exceed. I asked my clients to give me a week to mourn and get my mind right, as I am a book publisher. And after that week, I continued to work. But I started to notice that I was no longer fulfilled, that my passion for publishing was no longer there. I started to resent my difficult clients and so I knew it was time to level up. Although I was doing way better in my business during this pandemic than I had before, I felt an emptiness inside. When I was mourning, sad or just in a funk, I noticed that writing healed my soul and it has been like that since I was a child. I always had a passion for writing, but I never thought about making a career out of it. And although I was an author and publisher, I would ghostwrite books for my clients from time to time. And it hit me, or should I say God spoke to me and told me that this is something that I should do full-time.

And during this pandemic and this time of uncertainty, I converted my publishing company into a full ghostwriting business. When I decided to turn my pain into my passion and profit, the return was amazing. I marketed myself as a ghostwriter, and within 2 weeks, I had five ghostwriting clients. Writing is something I enjoy, and it is my passion to write for others. God gave me this gift and the means to level up in my career. I was able to travel to NYC to meet a client and be a guest at her book signing, I was able to pay off multiple debts and expand my business. Although we were hit with this pandemic and our world looks much different, as well as the fact that I had a major loss in my life and others have lost their lives, this still was not a bad year for me. God provided my family with everything we needed throughout this pandemic.

This is a historical time in our lives, and it humbled us to be appreciative of the people and the things that we have in our lives. I learned how to manage my money much better and how to appreciate the people and things in my life. This year has brought a lot of clarity to my life. I learned who was for me and who wasn't. The self-love, peace, and healing that I have over my life is priceless. And I have a dope angel watching over me.

I dedicate this chapter to my grandmother, my angel, Anna V. Triggs. Xoxo

"I can do all things through Christ who strengthens me."
(Philippians 4:13).

Award-winning and 7x Best Selling Author, Ghostwriter, and Publisher, Tanisha D. Mackin was born and raised in Buffalo, NY. **Phenomenal Women, 2016 Black Women Are award for survivorship**, the **2016 IALA award for Memoir of the Year** for her book, My Testimony, I Don't Look Like What I've Been Through, the **Women in the Spotlight Goin Global 2016 Rising Star Award**, the **2018 Best of McDonough, 2019 Business Hall of Fame** (Best of McDonough), the **ACHI Magazine 2019 Author of the Year Award**, the **2020 Business McDonough Hall of Fame and the 2020 Publisher Award**. She has worked on several books and book tours, including a book tour for Rhonda Henderson and 4x Grammy award-winning and reality star Stevie J. Tanisha became a #1 Best Selling Author with her eBook, What's Next, Sis? And with her book collaboration with Actress and Comedian Kim Cole.

Info.TanishaMackinPublishing@gmail.com
www.tanishamackin.com
IG: @TanishaMackinPublishing

7

Personal Pandemic

IS IT EVEN POSSIBLE TO prosper in a pandemic? Is God able to provide and set forth provision in the middle of what appears to be famine, loss, and disaster? The answer to those questions is a resounding, "yes!"

In March of 2020, I was abruptly dismissed from a new promising position, in the middle of training, almost one thousand miles from home. The entire class could feel that something wasn't right, the entire day felt "off." Actually, the last week leading up to the dismissal felt very strange. Things began to shut down all around us, like the cafeteria, meeting areas, and our hotels. The news was constantly projecting doom and gloom, and the amount of hand sanitizer available to us eerily increased. We were all alarmed, no doubt about it.

The most peculiar thing about experiencing all of this at the time I was experiencing it was that I was already in the middle of a "personal pandemic." My life completely changed a month before I left for training. I was finally able to cross paths with the career of my dreams. On the other hand, I was experiencing separation from my husband, along with a whirlwind of surmounting tough situations. It seemed like everything was piling up on me! I had already mustered up just enough strength to even pack and set my mind on going to a completely different state, as well as learning my new position. At the time, I did not know what was next, I was displaced and without surety in my life. I loved living a life that was solid, planned, sure, and stable. That all changed for me in February of 2020, and then it all changed indefinitely for the entire world in March of 2020.

Let's go back: I had prayed, posted (online), did vision boards, and journaled about my dreams and hopes of traveling for a living for many years. I started desiring a traveling career when I was in high school. It just seemed cool! Guys, I have an entire board on Pinterest entitled "World Traveler!" I am serious about traveling! Well, once we were released from training, the company was gracious enough to allow us who were dismissed to have the benefit of seeing the world for free. There was one huge problem with that, the world was "shutting down." We were all given this amazing benefit, but where would we go if we could not go anywhere? See the irony?

I returned back to my home state after a few days of debriefing and arriving at the realization of everything that happened. Once I returned home, it was so weird. The streets were empty. People were frightened, anxious, and scared. You could feel the fear; it was thick. Rumors of doom were flying, and the anxiety was high. Let's just talk about how spooky it was to depart from a major airport that was practically empty, and then to arrive at another major airport that was a ghost town as well. Y'all, it was just different and extremely scary.

I finally arrived home, and I began to write my first book; God had laid writing a book on my heart about fifteen years prior ("You Are Favor"). I started writing in April of 2020, and I was done by June of 2020. God literally lined up the publisher, editor, graphic designer, and the funds to complete the project seamlessly. I even had a successful book signing event in September of 2020. I threw my own party! I was determined to finish my very first book and celebrate the process as well! I had spent years doubting myself and my abilities, but God showed me once again what He could do with my "yes." I wrote my entire book on a very old tablet attached to a keyboard. It was one of those kinds of devices that you had to rig to work. The kind of machine that no one else would be able to properly use because there were so many "rigged" components that only you knew about. Nonetheless, I was determined to finish no matter what—no excuses allowed! I pushed through the inconvenience(s).

In June of 2020, I decided that I would begin to live in the abundance of no-cost travel, and I did! I have been to Mexico a few times—Dominion Republic, Key West, Charlotte, Atlanta, Chicago, Indianapolis, Baltimore, Phoenix, Jacksonville, Waycross, Houston, Raleigh-Durham, Dallas, and a host of other destinations, multiple times since June 2020. You don't see heavy overseas travel listed because I was determined to not live in fear, however, it was always my aim to remain safe. Now, if the world was truly "open," you would never see me! I would be sitting in the grass in Ireland for absolutely no reason and taking a million pictures while doing it! Although I have the ability to travel absolutely anywhere I desire, we are still in a pandemic. I am aware and ever so cautious, still.

Seeing that I was going through my own trials before the pandemic even began, I sought out extensive counseling once I returned home. I wanted to heal and heal properly, with guidance. Through that online counseling relationship, there have been so many new doors opened to me! New friendships, a new laptop, opportunities to travel and serve within the ministry, collaborations; I dove into my purpose, and re-launched my online boutique. Although I am not working a nine-to-five position, God has sustained me, blessed me with amazing family and friends, given me the freedom to travel, and has opened doors for me to write and be my authentic, creative self in this season.

The pandemic has presented the worst of times and the best of times, working simultaneously in my life. It is truly all working together for my good. God chose to elevate me and prosper me at the most peculiar time and in the most unique way. I got the chance to reset, as well as rest. God has been faithful! He just wants us to ensure that our hearts are properly postured towards Him. Learn all the lessons in the season you are in. Heal well and heal healthily. Determine within yourself to be a good steward in every circumstance, whether it be good or bad. His grace is enough for you!

II Corinthians 12:9 "My grace is all you need. My power works best in weakness." NLT

Andrea Renee' is a graduate of Eastern Michigan University with a Bachelor of Science degree in Communication. Her minor during undergrad was Journalism. Andrea is a passionate speaker and writer. Her goal is to actively encourage and uplift others through the Word of God and her own life experiences. Andrea believes that nothing is wasted, and everything that we go through is meant to assist us in growing and helping those around us. Andrea's goal is to inspire women and let them know that anything is possible through Christ. Purpose and love are what drive Andrea.

Andrea loves to travel, has an online fashion boutique, a blog, and a YouTube channel.

Author Contact: authorandrearenee@gmail.com

8

The Plot Twist

MARCH 18TH, 2020, my life shifted in a way I had not experienced before. My employer walked into my office and told me they needed to meet with me as soon as possible. I said okay, walked to their office, closed the door, and as they spoke, their words went mute. I was reading their lips but not hearing anything because fear gripped my heart. We received a letter from the Louisiana Dental Association. That is the board that makes the rules regarding the way dental offices and professionals can operate. The letter said that we needed to close our office effective immediately and until further notice. I could not speak. I could not move, but as one of the leaders of the practice, I had to put my feelings on pause for a moment. We gathered our team together and broke the news that we were shutting down and temporarily laying off everyone until further notice.

The looks on their faces broke my heart because they all had the same look of uncertainty, and I had no answers for them. I had no answers for myself. I called my husband, and as I was calling him, we were receiving messages from the schools regarding the boys, and the news was on the television in the lobby. Watching the uncertainty and fear in the face of our state leaders, educational leaders, spiritual leaders, and so many others was challenging. At that point, it still hadn't quite hit me what was going on until the following day, my alarm went off, but I had nowhere to go.

Around that same time, my first book was due to be released. I had, just a few months prior, joined forces with some amazing women to release an anthology. I was saying 20/20 vision; this was the year of the overflow. I said this is my year to be the head and not the tail, above and not beneath, the lender and no longer the borrower, right! God had other plans for me, though. I had been gearing up for this fantastic year without the full directions from God. I had my dreams mixed in with His plans, and that could not be so. God shut the world down for various reasons, but He needed to get my attention back for me. I had begun to lean into my abilities than depending on the one who gave them to me in the first place. My life was loud, and He needed me to get quiet and sit at His feet. I could not do that on the path I was gearing up to blaze once I realized what He desired from me, and that didn't happen initially. It was more like a few months of being angry, confused, and not wanting to pray. I was so caught up with how this could happen instead of seeking Him to understand what I needed to get out of it.

I did just that; I sat down and began to listen to what He was saying and where He was leading me. And before you knew it, I was on my way, this time following His plans. I had written two other anthologies, gained my speaking/coaching training and certification through John Maxwell. Found my niche, which is Leadership. I was able to become closer to my children because they had my undivided attention. My husband and I had deeper conversations because we had time. I thought I was winning before, but in the middle of a pandemic, in the middle of a crisis, I was genuinely winning! My relationship with God had grown stronger. I was happier about the woman that was emerging. God was not done yet. I could go back to the office a few weeks before everyone else, which means I was back to my salary sooner than anticipated. Once we were back, the team was doing better than we expected. Everywhere my feet tread and everything my hands touched prospered. In the middle of this, my husband contracted Covid.

I could have let this set me back, but in my time with God, I had come to the complete understanding that He is

God and He has us covered. He was extremely ill but did not have to go on a ventilator or be hospitalized. He was down for a while but recovered well and is as healthy as ever now. In all of those instances, the enemy thought he would keep me in a state of depression, in a state of fear. He thought he would win the war he had waged against my faith, but the PLOT TWIST was, my God is greater and more substantial. One of the scripture passages that kept me in the middle of the pandemic was 3 John 1: 2, "Beloved, I wish above all things that thou mayest prosper and be in good health, even as thy soul prospers." 2020 was the year this scripture came alive in my life.

I implore you to sit at His feet of the Father and listen to what He has to say. It will truly change your life! It did for me; I was able to prosper in the middle of a pandemic.

Teara Stewart is a best-selling author, international speaker, leader, and serial entrepreneur who resides in Louisiana with her husband and their three sons. Her mission in life is to create effective change in her community and in the lives of those around her.

Teara is the owner of The Leader Tree Consulting group, where the seeds to BE MORE takes root and are nurtured. She is also a practice manager for a dental office in Louisiana. She is a firm believer that the key to success is believing in yourself. Her faith in God is her guiding light on her journey.

"The mindset of the human being is a powerful tool so THINK responsibly" –Teara

You can reach her via email at:
emerge20@Yahoo.com
Facebook: facebook/teara.stewart.3
Instagram: tearastewart2011

9

The Journey to Discovering My Higher Self

AS I REFLECT ON THE YEAR 2020, I am truly grateful for the detours that changed everything. The pandemic brought both positive and negative changes to my family dynamics, yet nothing in comparison to the spiritual growth it provided for me. I was so excited to finally be able to do things independently, such as using my daily living skills, without waiting on someone to assist me. I know these all seem like simple tasks, and I would agree until I struggled each morning just to get out of bed and stand up on my feet. The emotional toll was more than overwhelming, as a mother of two, I had no plan for my own aftercare. I was so accustomed to taking care of others less fortunate than myself, now, who would I turn to for help.

I thank God for 2 amazing mothers, Ms. Liz and Ms. Sherren. I am thankful for their prayers and conversations while providing daily support during my recovery period. Hebrews 11:1 says, "Faith is the substance of things hoped for, the evidence of things not seen." I couldn't see my healing, but I had faith and proof that God still heals and delivers. I had no idea of the amount of stress I was carrying around, most of which didn't belong to me, it was external weights of about 80 pounds. Every so often a specialist would call and inquire about my mental and emotional health, which was helpful. To not be triggered or manage outbursts, she would say, "Allow yourself to process your thoughts and emotions." Most days, I wanted to scream, cry, break down, fall apart, but the question still remained in the back of my mind, "Who will take care of my kids." That one question was the fuel to push myself to learn as much as possible, to break free from any bondage I had allowed in my life because healing to return to work was my top priority, so I thought. There was a new normal being created before my eyes.

My first deliverance came shortly after the pandemic started, which was to be delivered from other people's opinions. I recall how humiliating it was to go from having enough to take care of my family to suddenly needing to ask for assistance after returning to work for less than half the pay. I frequently asked myself how I transitioned into this new existence while continuing to help the two families with their mother and uncle. One with dementia and the other a victim of a double stroke. For most of my life, I struggled with the word "transition or transitioning," as many times, it usually involved that person passing on into the afterlife. Strange as it may seem, caring for someone in the later stages in life is not for the faint at heart. In sharing some of my own struggles, as I was still using a walker and cane while helping them, many times the sacred space created during our conversations, outings, and meals, including them talking in circles or riddles as some of their family members would comment. But I could understand the messages they were attempting to share as I watched their anxiety build-up, and eventually, they would shut down or drift off into deep reflection. I would share my story of praying as a child to one day meet my biological father, to ask why I was so different than all of my siblings combined.

Well as the saying goes, "Be careful what you ask God for because you just might get it, just not like you imagined it to be." I was committed more than ever to work on my spiritual, mental, emotional, and physical health during the remaining time left on this earth. Quitting on life was not an option, once you see the dimming of the light in a person's eyes, you can never unsee it. All of my life, I watched my mom and father work all their life on a job that replaced them as their health began to fail. Although they could no longer perform their work duties, I witnessed them continue to provide shelter, support, and food to anyone in need. On my father's death bed, he shared a vision with me that I keep close to my heart. He said, "Kita, you see what you see and understand what you understand, you're not crazy. You have to help pull people out of the pits, it's time to stop hiding and show the world the real you!" That was the million-dollar question, who was I?

A woman that learned how to bury the pain and hurt of my silent cries until I lost myself in the illusion of being okay. I told myself, I just wanted to be free from my past hurts, disappointments, failures to myself, family, and community but struggling to show up as my highest self. That is when I started looking myself in the mirror and barely recognizing the person I was becoming. I still had much to learn about healing on an emotional and mental level. This required me to be open and honest in discussing my personal struggle with depression, betrayal, addictions, and rejection, by learning how to navigate through an overwhelming sea of emotions. What I discovered along the journey was that I was not alone, nor was my struggle permanent. Yes, I had to stop running away and face my fears one by one. Starting with the renewing of my mind, I gradually changed the voices I was listening to and what I was reading/watching; I noticed the more I began to feel and grow into a higher version of myself. Life demanded that I manage my emotions, build healthy relationships, to improve my character. I learned how to become a student of life by learning how to accept and appreciate how far I've traveled.

Nakita Haymer is a dedicated Arkansas mother of two and has a support dog "Stormi." She enjoys writing, reading, storytelling, and mentoring both women and children who need a helping hand back to the road of recovery. During the Covid-19 crisis of 2020, plagued with bills and illnesses, Nakita decided to reinvent herself by discovering how to share her life story to inspire and assist others with financial literacy education and created Kita's Kitchen in late 2020.

Nakita dedicates this chapter to her father's quote "You can't help anyone you're unwilling to touch." (Kenneth Gridley)

Contact information: nakitahaymer@gmail.com
https://www.facebook.com/2018isurvived

10

Stuck in a Dry Place

PRIOR TO THE PANDEMIC, I was working 80 hours a week, traveling from city to city with my job as a Program Coordinator auditing cases and training State employees on Federal mandates. I was operating a home-based baking business on the weekend that I started over 10 years ago. I knew I wanted to open a business but didn't know how I would accomplish it or who would assist me.

We were told that due to the pandemic, we would no longer be allowed to travel and would have to work from home. They also informed us that our workload would double, and the projected budget would not allow for the staff to receive a performance raise. Working with a staff that was depressed and frantic from the pandemic, I prayed and asked God to make a way out of no way because I knew that this was not going to work for me, and I wanted to get out.

I was led by the Holy Spirt to go and inquire about a vendor spot at our local Farmers Market that's located downtown. I had no knowledge of how this would work or what type of revenue this would produce. Keep in mind that I was already dealing with people all over the State with attitudes, and only God knows what it would be like to deal with customers. I obtained an application and the staff explained to me what was required and what time the vendors had to arrive to their assigned area. I contemplated this venture for over 3 months, and one morning, the Holy Spirit advised me to return the application. I was obedient and followed His instructions. I met with the director of the department, and she asked if I met all of the requirements that were needed. I showed her that I had a name for my business, my logo, and I had established a social media page for my home-based business. The director advised me that I would need to get a business license and meet the Health Department requirements.

At this point, I started thinking, is this something I want to do, it appeared that it was going to cost me more money and my purpose was to make money. I completed all of the requirements and returned to the office for the director to approve my application. She asked me if I had pictures of my work and I showed her my social media page. She advised me that most vendors at the market only rely on the customers that shop on Saturday morning, but I should do well with what she observed on my social media page. She went on to tell me that she had a special spot that had not been occupied in over a year due to owners not making enough money to cover the expenses.

We went into a space that was occupied with everything I could think of to bake every cake, cookie, and pie that my heart would desire. It was equipped with 2 windows for serving, a stove, an oven, a deep fryer, freezer, refrigerator, ice machine, and storage area. I cried because I knew that was nothing but God. I had prayed for a small business and didn't know how I was going to afford to buy the equipment that I needed to operate my business. She told me that I would need to submit a proposal to the mayor with my intentions for the space and I would need to wait for about 3 weeks before the unit would be ready for me to occupy if my proposal was approved. The director completed my proposal before I left her office that day. I started the next Saturday morning outside under the shed at 6:30 a.m. The preparation for this day almost killed me. I had to finish my day job with training and reports to start baking and packaging my items. I got 2 hours of sleep before I had to set up downtown. I was tired as ever and didn't know if I would make it. The director advised me that I had been approved and that made my morning. From 6 a.m. to 12 noon,

I had made over $300 selling cinnamon rolls, strawberry cream cheese rolls, and cake slices. At this point, I knew I could make it with my other customers that I had from over the years and with my new ones. I sat there in my seat and prayed and thanked God for what He was doing, but I knew this was just the beginning. As I was praying, the Holy Spirit spoke to me and said, "You now have a building that can be open 7 days a week if you choose to." I had to figure out now what days and hours I could work due to my other job. The Holy Spirit spoke again, "You do know you can cook food and bake." I opened up on that Sunday and called it Soul Food Sunday, working only on Saturday and Sunday for the next 2 months. God sent me a person to bless me financially and my business has been blessed. I had to struggle with what to put on my menu and think about what population I would be serving. I developed a menu that was suitable for everyone, from smoothies, salads, sandwiches, and veggie alternatives. God allowed me to resign from my job that I worked for over 17 years with the State, to pursue my passion for cooking. It has been a year later, and God has shown up for me once again in the midst of a global pandemic, allowing me to open another restaurant at the airport in my hometown. I advised everyone not to get discouraged by small beginnings. John 14:13-14, "And whatsoever ye shall ask in my name, that will I do, that the Father may be glorified in the Son."

Evangelist Shelia Aaron is a native of Denmark, TN. She is the proud mother of two children, her daughter Jessica Taylor and son Jared Taylor. Ms. Aaron is the founder of Sacrifice, a nonprofit organization that was developed in 2014 to encourage and engage individuals. She was ordained as a minister in 2018, where she serves as a mentor within the community. Ms. Aaron is now the owner of Shelia Sweet Secrets bakeshop and restaurant, located in downtown Jackson, Tn. Cooking has always been a part of her life, and during the pandemic, she was able to share her love of cooking with the community. Ms. Aaron is an Alumni of Union University, where she received a master's degree in the field of social work. Ms. Aaron retired from the Tennessee Department of Children Services as a Program Coordinator in the accreditation department after 17 years.

11

Partner in Christ: Bound to Freedom

ON SEPTEMBER 6, 2018, I was fired before I clocked in from a place where I overworked myself and spent two years of my life. YES! I was *Fired Before Work*. I was shocked that out of ALL the people that were there and should've been fired, I was like the first to go. It made me realize that no matter how much I wanted to stay or how comfortable I was, if God is telling you to move, THEN MOVE! or He will find a way and do it for you. I didn't get fired at the hands of man; I got pushed out and promoted by the plans of The All-Knowing God.

Wwwhhaaaatt? Now I'm a full-time entrepreneur by force. Yes, I have always wanted to be a full-time entrepreneur, but I wanted to do it at my own pace and whenever I had more clarity, time, and money. In all actuality, I was fearful and in my comfort zone. But let me tell you, our ways and plans are not like God's plans (Proverbs 19:21; Isaiah 55:8-9). Can I get a witness? Right after being fired from my "J.O.B.," everything seemed to go well, I wrote my very first book *Fired Before Work*, I spoke on radio shows, I closed a real estate deal (then stopped), I created and sold products, I did side hustles, I was able to just get up and go on vacation without having to request time off. I was also able, through my experience, to help, encourage, motivate, and change other people's lives. I did some of the things that I was taught and knew to do in order to survive. I knew I couldn't and didn't want to go back to a 9 to 5 after being fired. Even though I had accomplished those great things over a two-year time span, I was now in 2020 during a global pandemic, also trying to, number one, balance me secretly breaking down, and number two, being strong for others and a shining light in this dark real world.

Life looked good from the outside looking in. I used to always hear things like, "Girl, you got it going on," "You're strong," "You killin' it," etc. But deep down, on the inside, I was struggling to make it. I was BOUND in my mind. I was bound by fear, the opinions of others, self-limitations, then I became bound by this sneaky thing called depression. Whew! It was like I was in prison without bars. I wasn't doing so good financially, sales started decreasing and decreasing and decreasing, people weren't really supporting me. My money started to dry up. It felt like I was in a drought... the wilderness with no rain, maybe a drop here and a drop there, a sprinkle here and a sprinkle there. But one thing I didn't lose was my praise. And I want to encourage you, even in the midst of trouble, don't lose your praise. I prayed and prayed and cried out to the Lord, asking Him, what's going on, screaming in my shower, "HHH-HEEELLLPPP LORD, HELP ME, I'M IN DESPERATE NEED OF YOUR HELP."

I knew I was supposed to have more. I knew I was supposed to be in a better state than I was in. I was literally in a spiritual warfare. It may have been invisible, but it was indeed POWERFUL and tried to take me out. Day in and day out, I slept; I felt like I didn't know my purpose again. I was so confused in my mind to where I didn't know what task to start on. I didn't know whether to sleep or get up and try to work on something. I thought so little and didn't feel good about myself and where I was currently at in life. I saw other people prosper and make sales, I heard other people get their prayers answered. And there I was STILL BOUND, down and depressed.

"Why hasn't God answered me? Why hasn't God given me instruction? Why haven't I seen a shift in my finances and business?" All these questions I was asking and expecting an answer to. But it seemed as if I was getting NO answer. I was out there by myself (so I thought), not even God was answering me. I was in a fight by myself, getting beaten and bruised. If I had killed myself, no one would've known because I didn't have people check on me except maybe two people. "God, where is everyone at?" Have you ever felt so alone? "Why am I going through this?" Fast forward: I went on a fast and I was sad because I was expecting God to give me something big and new during the fast, but realized I was in the place I was in because of **disobedience** (sin, Romans 6:23). Death was around me, not physically, but in other areas, due to me being disobedient. I had to lay aside the sin, according to Hebrews 12:1, and repent for my disobedience. (Pause: Take an evaluation of your life. Why are you where you are today?)

So, all this time of me going through being depressed, etc. I could have been out had I made a conscious choice to be free and accept the freedom (God's way) that was already there. I had to let go! I chose to be bound (by way of disobedience). I got deceived, thinking I was free, but I was only free in a cage. I was once bound trying to become free, now I have Partnered in Christ, repenting and accepting His way of doing things. Now I'm bound to freedom. Make a decision today to be free and say, "I AM FREE, PRAISE THE LORD I'M FREE. I'M NO LONGER BOUND. NO MORE

CHAINS HOLDING ME. MY SOUL IS RESTING, AND IT'S SUCH A BLESSING. PRAISE THE LORD, HALLELUJAH, I'M FREE."

Jerrica Brumfield, an Accountability Coach from a small town called Picayune, MS. On September 6, 2018, being fired from her job unexpectedly became the start of a new life as a full-time entrepreneur. During the first year of her being fired, she became an Author and a Self- publisher of her book, Fired Before Work, in less than 30 days.

She is very passionate about helping others gain clarity, discover their gifts and talents, and use them to create businesses and earn extra income. She is based online at www.jerricabrumfield.com and jkb.bigcartel.com

She is also known for motivating, encouraging, and pulling greatness out of those who come in contact with her.

Jerrica is here to be the hope and restoration to this world, one person at a time.

IG: @Jerrica_Brumfield
FB: @Jerrica "Jredd" Brumfield

12

"How the Pandemic Changed my Mindset and My Life."

GROWING UP, WE ALL HAD DREAMS. Many of which we had no clue of how much hard work it would take to get there. But we didn't care. All we saw was the big picture. It didn't matter if what we dreamed of becoming didn't make any logical sense. We were optimists, excited, and very confident that we would succeed in accomplishing those dreams. Until someone or something comes along and bombards us with their opinions/knowledge about how the world works and why we can/can't accomplish our dreams. In some instances, light and love are poured into the child, giving them the support and confidence that they need to pursue their dreams. In other instances, fear and discouragement are spoken into them and their dream becomes unrealistic or unattainable to them. Well, the latter is exactly what happened to me. As a child, I was talked out of following my dreams of becoming an author. As time progressed, no matter what field of study I chose, it was never good enough for those that were my support system or to those that I looked to for support.

After many failed attempts at other careers over the years, the urge to write was always there. I couldn't shake it no matter how much I tried. So, in 2017, for the first time in years, I picked up my pen and started writing again. I felt the need to tell my story about how I allowed the opinions of others to affect and change the way I would live my life. I wanted to help others change their mindset and live the life of their dreams. I was a people pleaser for years and the time came when I was finally tired of living my life for others. I began writing. However, all of those years of worrying about other people's opinion was in the back of my mind until the Pandemic hit in 2020. With life as we knew it now completely changed, I saw so much fear and uncertainty in the eyes of others. No one seemed secure or sure of anything anymore. It seems all hope was lost in their eyes, and defeat was right around the corner. This thought shook me to my core, and I asked myself, "What is life with no hope in it?" I couldn't imagine that, and I most definitely did not want others to continue to live life feeling that way. So, I felt I had to do something.

Since I was already in the process of writing my book about changing one's mindset, I felt this was the best way to give hope and a way for others to change their situations through changed thinking. One only needs to follow three simple steps to create a mindset change. First, have clarity about what you want and the life you envision for yourself. Second, set precise intentions of how you will change your thought process towards your circumstances. Lastly, commit to taking actionable steps to change your mindset and your circumstances.

During the process of finalizing my book, I felt the urge to do more. I couldn't just give guidance on how to change one's mindset without giving some type of ongoing support or mentoring. I wanted others to be able to come to me for help well after they purchased my book. I wanted to create a community of like-minded individuals, who all wanted the same thing, to change their mindset, create a better life for themselves, and create hope for a better future regardless of their current situations. So, I started my business in August 2020 called The Change Strategy, LLC. I finished and published my book, and I am now preparing to offer courses on implementing the Change Strategy in a variety of areas in people's lives. I don't want to be a one-time motivator. I am working to be a lifetime teacher of change! My passion to help others allowed me to achieve my dream regardless of the hardship the pandemic has brought. The old way of life has gone, and our new way of life has begun. The pandemic changed everything, but I am here to make a change for the better! With you, I leave this message. Regardless of your circumstances, having a positive mindset will allow you to create a positive vision and plan for your future.

With all of that being said about what I do, who exactly am I? Born and raised in Varnado, Louisiana, my name is Paula A. Harrison, and I am the owner of The Change Strategy, LLC and the author of the book "The Change Strategy: Change your thinking, change your life." I currently reside in Hattiesburg, Mississippi with my husband and three children. I am an up-and-coming mindset coach and motivational mentor, where I focus on changing negative thinking and habits and reframe them into positive thinking and habits. I am also a paralegal for a private firm, notary public, and social media marketing manager. I have an Associate of Applied Business Office Technology/Legal Assisting and Associate of Applied Science in Marketing and Social Media Management. I am currently working on my second book called "Changed Habits with Positive Reframing."

To keep up with future projects, follow me on Facebook.com/thechangestrategy and Instagram.com/thechangestrategy. You can also visit my website at www.the-change-strategy.com or shoot me a quick email at coaching.tcs@gmail.com.

Matthew 6: 25-26

[25] *"Therefore I tell you, do not worry about your life, what you will eat or drink; or about your body, what you will wear. Is not life more than food, and the body more than clothes?* [26] *Look at the birds of the air; they do not sow or reap or store away in barns, and yet your heavenly Father feeds them. Are you not much more valuable than they?"*

Paula A. Harrison is the owner of the Change Strategy, LLC and the author of *The Change Strategy: Change Your Thinking, Change Your life*. She is a paralegal by day and a mindset coach by night. She received her Associate of Applied Business Office Technology/Legal assisting degree and Associates of Applied Science in Marketing and Social Media Management degree at Antonelli College of Hattiesburg, Mississippi.

Native of Angie, Louisiana, and currently residing in Hattiesburg, Mississippi, Paula lives with her husband, three kids, two dogs, and a talkative cat. She is a lover of journaling, animals, and books. If you want to know more about what Paula offers at the Change Strategy, please visit her website at www.the-change-strategy.com where you can sign up to receive email updates. You can also follow her on Facebook @thechangestrategy and Instagram @thechangestrategy.

13

Living Life in Purpose

IN 2020, THERE WAS SOMETHING that changed the USA as we knew it. It was COVID-19. COVID-19 changed things for me. Before COVID-19 ever came, I had been struggling with finding peace about some situations in my life; I had been praying and asking God to change me, to direct my steps, and help me to live my life on purpose. I didn't want to do anything if there wasn't purpose in it. I wanted to stop procrastinating. So, in January of 2020, I found myself re-writing my vision for Refuge of Hope, Inc. Before I could get things going, we were in a lockdown. Businesses were working from home, laying people off, city and county had a curfew, places you could go was limited. There was a shortage of household items, and you were limited to what you could get.

I didn't have a time during the pandemic that I lacked in anything. God started blowing my mind from the beginning. When I would go to get supplies, groceries, etc. I always got what I needed. And a lot of times I was able to get things for others. Even when it came down to my job, I lacked in nothing. June of 2020, I actually received a very nice raise. There again God was showing me that when you prove faithful to Him, and the work He has called you to do, you lack nothing, and He proves Faithful. God had increased my financials so that I was able to help others, that had been impacted by COVID-19. I am reminded of this scripture, Luke 6:38 KJV: Give, and it shall be given unto you; good measure, pressed down, and shaken together, and running over, shall men give into your bosom. For with the same measure that ye mete withal it shall be measured to you again."

November of 2020, right before Thanksgiving to some, what was the worst thing that could happen, happened to me. I contracted COVID-19. Yet, I was still thankful to God because I wasn't hospitalized; I didn't lose my life. Yes, I had symptoms and it didn't feel good at all, and I had some side effects that still affect me now, but God! I won't complain. I recovered. During those few weeks that I was recovering, laying in my bed, I began to reflect on the prayers that I had before God last year. In the midst of me having COVID-19,

God began showing me what He had purposed for my life. See I had been so busy with work, life, and doing what I thought was important to me that I couldn't hear the voice of God. God has a way of getting our attention. That peace, and direction that I was so desperately looking for, I began to get while lying flat on my back. I had been stretching myself so thin, and not having balance in my life. God began to show me in this pandemic that my life had purpose, and if I would only just rest in Him, everything would be fine. I was so consumed with what others thought of me, and what others wanted me to do. But then I started believing that I had purpose and that during this pandemic, God was going to do something mighty in me.

At first, I began to wonder, and even question if what I desired could happen in the midst of this crisis, but then I was reminded of all the things that God had brought me through in my life, and He had never broken a promise to me. I began to understand in this season of my life that when you live in purpose, that's the best life to live. I stopped worrying about what others thought of me and started believing what God was showing and telling me. Some days, God will literally say, "Girl you have purpose, get up. What are you waiting on?" Every prayer, every desire God answered, and it wasn't because I was so good. I messed up and made mistakes. I questioned Him when I shouldn't have, and I always didn't understand. If I was asked the question, what did you learn in this pandemic, I would say that I learned to depend on God, no matter what the circumstances look like. I learned that people will let you down and turn their backs on you. But God's love for you will never fail. So often we walk away from God, but He never leaves us. I learned the biggest lesson, and that was no matter what the enemy or people try to make me think, my life has purpose and meaning.

I would like to leave with you this scripture, Jeremiah 29:11: "For I know the thoughts that I think toward you, saith the Lord, thoughts of peace, and not of evil, to give you an expected end." No matter what state the world is in, or no matter what the circumstances look like, we have an expected end with God. Only God could move mountains in a pandemic. Only God could bless you to go without any lack, and to birth what others thought was dead in you. I'll say keep your hands in God's hand and watch Him change the universe.

Demetria L. Baker is a proud wife of Lewis Baker, and mother to De'Nitria L. Robinson, and Tyvon N. Munnings. She is also a minister, boss, entrepreneur, author empowerment coach, and Founder and CEO of Refuge of Hope, Incorporated. A non-profit organization that empowers individuals and brings healing and restoration. Demetria has a career in banking and finance; she has been blessed to be CEO of Lynchburg Municipal Employees Federal Credit Union since 2018.

Demetria has a passion for outreach and community service. Her most rewarding community service is when she can visit the Domestic Violence Shelters and talk or assist women in whatever need they have. Demetria herself is a survivor of domestic violence, her greatest mission is to let women know they can Speak Out.

To connect with Demetria, visit her on Facebook. Demetria L. Baker, Refuge of Hope, Inc, or A Journey to Healing Empowering Coaching.

14

Sanity Ever After
A Mind Prepared to Prosper

DURING THIS HISTORIC EVENT, a global pandemic, we all were faced with subsequent challenges. With everything that transpired in a year's time, you were either affected physically, financially, emotionally, or mentally. Many lost jobs, homes, loved ones, they maybe even lost themselves. But I thank God that in the midst of all this, a single mother, unemployed, pregnant, and fighting the constant battle of my mind, I was blessed to overcome it all and was graced to walk in my Sanity Ever After.

One of the greatest challenges for me was to accept the fact that I suffered from a mental disorder. In the beginning, I suffered in shame and silence. Constantly contemplating on the thoughts of "How could I, a daughter of the Most High, a part of the chosen generation, a royal priesthood, be mentally unstable? Why did this bloodline stigma have to affect me? I'm supposed to have the mind that is in Christ Jesus!" But in all actuality, according to my diagnosis, I am the total opposite. Make it make sense! I tried to keep myself busy by attending church regularly, cooking and catering from home to provide for my children, and being an overly extended helping hand to others. I even attempted to self-medicate with marijuana and alcohol, addictions I picked up as a teenager, that followed me into adulthood. These I used to keep myself calm, and for that moment, allowed me to block the feelings of all the trauma from my past and present experiences.

Eventually, these unhealthy tactics were no longer able to sustain me. Unfortunately, in the public eye, I crashed and burned. As hurtful and humiliating as it was, it wasn't until my now third nervous breakdown that I knew I had to do something different. I knew that PTSD, schizophrenia, anxiety, depression, and bipolar disorder were not my identity nor portion. I wanted my children to experience their mother healthy and whole. I wanted to be the woman who God created and called me to be in the spirit and in the natural. I now knew that what God had revealed, I had to now deal with and heal from.

Accepting this ugly truth about my life was one of the best things I never knew I needed to truly prosper. Once

God allowed me to become comfortable with being transparent about my struggles internally and externally, it shifted my perspective from struggle to strength. I have to be honest and tell you, this was not an overnight process. My mind had to be totally recalibrated, and everything I once knew about my life had to be restructured. The road to recovery began with several sessions in a lounge chair and many hours of intensive prayer! The safe place of a listening ear, and a strategic unfiltered prayer life, allowed me to pick up the pieces and rebuild my life! The more consistent I became in prayer, the more God began to restore me, establish me, and color all the gray areas according to His perfect plan and divine destiny for my life.

My posture in prayer shifted my position in the natural as well as in the spirit. When I became fully functioned in my healing, it was as if God Himself had a highlight on me and everything concerning me. My "breathe again season" was here, I could see clearly and literally feel the fresh winds blowing. My prayers began to manifest one by one. God set order, not one area in my life could be lukewarm but fueled by fire! I had to let all my Yes be Yes and my No's be No! Reconciliation and healing hit my family and me like never before. We began to understand each other thoroughly, communicated more effectively, and then loved and enjoyed each other's company.

Divine connections suddenly showed up. I was introduced to a group of phenomenal women of faith, true purpose pushers, handpicked, anointed, and appointed, who helped birth my first steps from poverty to promise. These ladies lifted me up in prayer and brought forth strategies for success in spirit and in truth. Their wisdom and transparency caused the demons of guilt, shame, and self-doubt to be slain. For my leadership in my community, I was later chosen to be in a quarterly initiative program designed for low-income single mothers by the name of Magnolia Mothers Trust through Springboard to Opportunities, which provided a monthly stipend of $1,000 for one year. Unemployed and a now soon-to-be single mother of four children, this opportunity allowed me to self-sufficiently meet the needs of my household as well as invest in building my brand and business. I gave birth to a handsome baby boy that came into the world perfectly healthy and happy! Even in the midst of a pandemic, where family was limited, I was blessed to have an outstanding labor and delivery team. Everyone was patient, safe, and yet again women and men of faith! I had now learned that when you are truly chosen and a child of the Most High, He'll go before you and make every crooked path straight. It blessed me beyond measure to know that God always had and always will care about the things concerning me. For this very reason, I'm honored to carry out the roles of an Overcomer, Generational Curse Breaker, and More than a Conqueror!

Today, as a walking, talking testimony, I leave you with this, pain never comes without purpose being attached to it! Never be so afraid of change that you don't. Humiliation is sometimes one of God's strategies to humble and to usher us into showing compassion for others whose struggle may not necessarily look like ours! Allow yourself to progress in your process, you may be next in line for the Blessing! It was this wisdom that turned me from 'who is she' to 'there she is' because "I can do all things through Christ which strengthens me," Philippians 4:13 and "We know that [with great confidence] that God [who is deeply concerned about us] causes all things to work together [as a plan] for good for those who love God, to those who are called according to His plan and purpose, Romans 8:28 AMP. Today I thank God for my SANITY EVER AFTER!

Brianne' Epps is a woman of faith, mother of four beautiful children, infant and toddler teacher, and caterer. She resides in Jackson, MS where she advocates the success and self-sufficiency of single mothers and fathers in the areas of faith, finance, and mental health. Brianne' has always enjoyed encouraging and feeding everyone she met. By the time she was 25, she had reached many in her community through encouraging words and hearty meals. Brianne' began a home-based catering business and a non-profit organization. Now she is the owner and incorporator of Prayers Plates & Purpose Catering LLC and Mothers on the Move and Fathers out Front Incorporated. When she's not working with children, food, or her nonprofit, she loves to write poetry/short stories, sitting by the water for relaxation and inspiration, and spending intimate time with her children. As purpose-driven as she is, she humbly walks daily in her Pit to Palace experience. She strives to make Jesus famous again for his divine healing power and ability to make those who were last at the anointed and appointed time first.

15

During the Pandemic

IT STARTED TOWARD THE end of 2019 when I felt the Lord leading me to go back to school. It had been seven years since I graduated with my master's, and I was getting frustrated with my financial situation. I felt like my master's degree was not making an impact on my check each month (I'm a school teacher). The Lord led me to the University of West Georgia where I was accepted into the Instructional Technology program. It had been so long since I was in school that I forgot to register for my classes and missed the deadline. My classes were closed out, and to be honest, I was relieved. I said to myself, "Well Lord, I guess I can't go to school!" The VERY NEXT DAY, my advisor emailed me and said the classes reopened and I needed to register. I was mad because I didn't want to go back to school even though I knew I needed to; I just didn't want to because I was over school at this point.

I started classes in January 2020, and I loved them. It was a lot of work, but I was learning so many things. I even redesigned my entire classroom teaching style to incorporate more technology and my students loved it. They were technologically inclined, and these changes really benefitted them. I told my principal at the time, and she said to me, "Remember technology can NEVER replace direct instruction." A month later, schools were shut down for Coronavirus. I will never forget that moment. I always wondered if she thought about that. While the country was shut down, I felt the Lord leading me to write an e-book. I sat through an online class hosted by Alandria Lloyd on how to create an e-book and sell them, and I believe I wrote that e-book in two days.

Around April of 2020, I felt the Holy Spirit leading me to begin looking for a house. I had been living with my parents since I graduated from college in 2009, and I was beyond ready to move. Usually, every year during the Daniel fast my church does in January, I make a prayer list of things to pray about for the year. Every year, I wrote, "own my own home." For the Daniel Fast 2020, I didn't include that. I know the Word says to "Ask and you will receive" (Matt. 21:22). "Ask...seek...knock..." (Matt. 7:7). "Have faith in God" (Mark 11:22). I knew the Lord knew I wanted to move. However, I had learned to be content in that current situation (Phil. 4:11). I knew that when I delighted myself in the

Lord, He would give me the desires of my heart (Ps. 37:4), because my will would be whatever His will would be for me. The Lord sent me one of the best realtors ever through my close friend, her brother. He was patient and knows the Lord.

While all of this was going on, I was having a rough time at my job. There was no outward opposition, but internally I was battling. I was having growing pains because my spirit knew it was time for me to move. I applied for a high school special education position at a school where I graduated from, knew the principal, where I used to work. I thought I was a shoe-in. No. No, I was not hired there, but I received a call in the early hours of a June morning, asking if I wanted to interview for a position at the other high school that had been on the website for a while, that I refused to apply for. I interviewed that same day and was hired. I was already working on my solo book that Alandria was helping me with, but I kept putting it off. The Lord sat me down while I was on summer break the week before the manuscript was due, and the Holy Spirit fell on me so heavily one evening, I completed that book in a matter of hours. In July, there was an open house on a townhome/condo that I viewed, and on September 4th, I closed on my home!

In March 2021, I turned the title of my book into the name of my business, Blessed Is She That Believed, LLC because when I received the first copy of my book, the Lord told me it wasn't just a book, it is a brand. I use everything that I am in school for to operate my business. I make websites from scratch, and I help small businesses get their social media pages up and running. I think about my life and how everything, EVERYTHING I went through, is being used RIGHT NOW for and to the glory of the Lord! I am amazed at how the trials and trauma I went through, He turned them around for my good just like He said He would!

I went to pick up food with a friend at the beginning of the shutdown. While I was waiting for my food, a lady who worked there came from the kitchen and began to prophesy over me. I don't usually let everyone pray for me, but I felt the Holy Spirit leading me to listen to her. I cannot remember everything she said, but she said to me, "...because people thought they were taking advantage of you, but you gave from a willing heart the Lord is about to answer your grandmother's and your mother's prayers through you. You are about to receive blessing after blessing like a ripple effect. People are going to ask you 'Didn't the Lord just bless you, and didn't you just get this?'..." About a month after I purchased my home, the Lord blessed me to purchase a brand-new vehicle. I saw someone a few weeks later and she said, "Didn't you just buy a home? Wait. You have a truck now? But I thought..."

Stephanie R. Cooper is a native of Southeast Georgia. She is currently working as a high school English teacher. She is actively involved in her church working in the technology ministry. Stephanie is completing her Ed.S in Instructional Technology and will graduate at the end of summer 2021. Stephanie is a published author. She has shared her testimony in "Dear Young Woman: There is Triumph After the Trial" and the follow-up "Dear Young Woman: Readjust Your Crown." Stephanie has two independent books under her name. Her first released e-book, "Until the Wait Is Over: When Will My Season Come" and her newly released solo book "Blessed Is She That Believed" which are all on her website: www.blessedisshethatbelieved.com.

16

Fight the Power

WE HAVE THREE ENTITIES THAT drive us with our thoughts, decisions, and actions. The Lord Jesus Christ, the enemy, and ourselves. God's sweet voice, blessings, protection, and ever-loving grace and mercy awakens us because, without a shadow of a doubt, we can stand bold in it. Chaotic mess, hate, evil intentions, everything that shows to be difficult and uncomfortable is nothing but the devil. But how do we identify, or better yet, when do we take accountability for knowing whether we are faced with God or the enemy traits in our lives. Maybe it's neither. Maybe it's you.

I recently had an "a-ha moment" where I can no longer stomach the life that is called mine. A single mother, running the show in the house, while dealing with everyday life and things that come up suddenly. I mean whether on their own or not, mothers all over the world know this feeling all too well. I also call myself carrying other people's mess!! Every other day, I'm frustrated to the point where it throws my whole mood and day off. When I do get the luxury to have quiet time, I find myself overextending myself the whole day. I have a list of things that need to get done in my head, alerts from my phone ready to go. I encourage myself to find some energy to get up and get going. Unfortunately, depression wins at times. Now the question is, why would I allow myself to feel this way, and why let this up and down rollercoaster go on for so long? Well, this is when I faced the harsh reality that I do not cherish and love on myself as much as I thought I did.

During this revelation moment from God, He told me, "Yes, it was indeed the enemy running amuck in my life, but I was allowing him to." We do not intentionally say, "Hey devil! Let's work together to cause chaos today wherever you see fit. Make yourself comfortable and have fun. See you later!" Absolutely not, but how we speak of and see ourselves is automatic grounds on whether your day comes with peace or dysfunction. I went down a list of everything that happens throughout my day to see what should stay, what needs to change, and what needs to go. I was fine until I got a pattern, but this time, I started to get uncomfortable. This area of my life has no boundaries. Listen, I tolerate a lot of difficult people who are battling their own demons. But that's all I've known, where it has become a normalcy, not easily to be detected.

God has chosen me to be one of the generational curse breakers in my family. This thing is tough, but yet so rewarding. I promise you, if it wasn't for God providing the manual for this, I would've thrown in the towel a while ago. He created me to be on this assignment, so I'm going all the way until my work is done. Throughout my life, one of the most damaging traits I have developed is psychological warfare. Verbal abuse, emotional abuse, control spirits, and victimization resulted in creating a person outside of myself who wanted to belong in order to shield myself from the blows. All I wanted to do was please people so I would not be condemned for the smallest thing. All the while, I just wanted to run. I knew what was occurring wasn't right. Is this my fault, no. Just like the scripture says that what the enemy meant for evil, God meant it for good (Genesis 50:20), it was now up to me to do something about this.

As a child of God, I was never promised "singing and laughing in a field of sunflowers" every day. The enemy would always and forever be trying it, but with and in God, I have power and authority over anything that comes up against my destiny, calling, and the promises that He has for me. When I don't remember who I am in God, decreed and declared over myself daily, that gives the enemy legal permission to come and place his plans of attack wherever he sees fit. Those spiritual curses I endured caused me to have triggers where I get angry and show my tail with these certain persons. Knowing that their fight is not really with me but among themselves, I could never decipher what was personal because the anguish was already planted. One day, I had a conversation with someone near and dear to my heart. It was after I had become angry and upset with someone who constantly triggers me no matter my position of faith in them. I told her that I should believe that THIS is what I have to deal with my entire life. She stated, "I do not, but I do because I do not know boundaries." Hold on, a minute! I can have boundaries with this person. I mean, you would think I would know this already, which I do, BUT anytime I mustered up the strength to place these boundaries, however, they looked, I was made to be wrong. I had to tolerate them because of who they were to me.

No title in this world should be given a pass to display abuse of any kind towards you. Anyone who believes this is someone who gets uncomfortable when they can no longer be the victim. It is time to fight that power and stand in the power which comes from the Lord. This is not so much the promise of God but the revelation that then propels you to that promise. Be mindful that without understanding and growing during the process with God, causes the beauty of stagnation. I pray my transparent words, with God's teachings, not only bless you but also give you strength to fight.

Psalm 121

Nyisha Beverley is a rising author with the mission to provide authenticity of transparency and testimonies that will impact lives. She holds an associate degree in social sciences and is currently obtaining her Bachelor of Arts in Psychology with a minor in African American Studies.

Her hope is to use her educational background to advocate in minority communities the importance of resources and knowledge to combat the mental health crisis. She also sees the importance of breaking generational curses to propel the strength of the community.

A mother of one, Beverley takes pride in preparing and dominating her destiny to leave her legacy thriving for generations to come. For contact information, email her at nybeverley@gmail.com and on Instagram @nybeverley.

17

Pivot. Position. Prosper

2020 IS MY YEAR!

Well, that's what I proclaimed! Myself and many others I know. We even had vision boards and girl gatherings in 2019 to discuss exactly how it would go. I knew If I did exactly what I did for my clients and myself last year, with just a few minor tweaks, with less procrastination, and firing on all cylinders, 2021 would be a piece of cake! My goal was to earn $5 Million, author ten books, mentor 20 clients to $100k in 6-12 months, launch three new revenue-generating platforms, invest in real estate, travel to Croatia, Paris, and Dubai, just to name a few. I had BHAGs (Big Hairy Audacious Goals)!

NEWSFLASH: March 13, 2020: President Donald Trump declared a U.S. national emergency, and on March 15th, the CDC warned against large gatherings of 50 or more.

WAIT! I'm "THE Bottomline Queen." I crush mediocrity! I multiply the revenue and profits of entrepreneurs and small business owners! I mentor, coach, train, teach, speak, network, brunch, dinner and gather for a living!

I must admit, initially, I was devastated but remained hopeful. "This shouldn't last for more than a few weeks," I thought. However, 48 hours later, on March 17th: the virus was present in all 50 states, and every day, there were new discoveries and even more restrictions. Even though I was frustrated and in disbelief, I remembered a billionaire mentor saying, "Tina, if you want to become wealthy, find out where the world is going and get there during the first wave. You don't have to be first, just get there. When you do that, you will never have to worry about money again! Simply BE the solution to a need!"

PIVOT: I was invited to a Zoom conference call hosted by a top nephrologist who called on community leaders, influencers, healthcare providers, and pastors. I have a genuine concern and compassion for people and am trained as a Physician Assistant, so I was "in the room!" I wanted to donate my services in any capacity. On approximately our third call, one of the medical clinic administrators stated that they and other clinics needed masks and other medical supplies. I went from listening intently as a participant to interrupting the conversation, as a moderator, requesting his contact information, assuring him that I could fulfill the order and would call him afterward. Under normal circumstances, I would say, I have no idea "why" or "where" that came from, but as a faith walker, I simply trusted God.

In the midst of the "pandemic" and all the discoveries about the virus, physicians, first responders, healthcare workers, and the American people felt scared and unsafe. Protective gear such as masks, gloves, eye gear, facial protective shields, hand sanitizer, alcohol pads, surgical gowns, and many other medical supplies was extremely scarce and in high demand. No one expected a pandemic, so stocks were insufficient, and no shipments from overseas were admitted into the United States (especially China because that was where the "virus" was said to have originated).

POSITION: We did some research, made a few phone calls, and by the grace of God, Protective Gear Unlimited was birthed! It was a challenge to procure the merchandise, but we prevailed. We had masks, gloves, face shields, and gowns. June 2020, the number of people who had contracted the virus reached 2 million! Our economy remained strained and shut down as 22 million Americans were unemployed. (Praise Break) Amid a pandemic, I was able to position myself and my business to thrive. With just two orders from the clinics, more than half of my year's income was replaced. HALLELUJAH!

As the world began to accept that wearing masks, facial protective clothing, working from home, and virtual meetups were the norm, many entrepreneurs and business owners realized they needed to pivot. Mastering strategies, blueprints, launches, webinars, and collaborations to replace the lost income first and then supersede that, was a priority. There's nothing like having the expertise and skillset to build a system that would provide CPR to a financially choking entity! It's my superpower!

PROSPER: You see, I had made my plans, wrote them in ink, and was ready to execute, but God prepared something different. Not only did He have a ram in the bush, but He also provided a vehicle where I earned almost $50,000 in 60 days. That's not even the best part. I was also able to help my friends and clients earn income too! Yes! Even during an economic debacle! (Praise dance and shuffle right here!)

It has been FULL STEAM AHEAD. Even though I'm trained as a healthcare professional, a PA, I discovered very early on that I was chronically unemployable. I worked at a clinic, and while working there, I started a housekeeping service which was my first taste of entrepreneurship. I was smitten and have had numerous businesses ever since. Some were a bust, others were profitable, and the later ones were explosive! I have a gift, and I don't take it for granted. I can take any business model, from a lemonade stand, a makeup artist, a teacher, a nurse, a speaker, an author, a printing shop to a Fortune 100, 500, or 5000 company and drastically multiply its revenue and profit margin (if I can't create a blueprint or strategy to enhance your bottom line, then there is none). I've been called the "Cash Flow Catalyst" by the Small Business Expo, the Queen of Rapport & Recruiting, an Expert, and even a Magician. As long as the results are substantiated, I'll take it!

I know it's uncomfortable in this season. You may be terrified, or maybe you're thriving. The bottom line is, where do you go from here? If you don't know. Let me tell you! UP! No matter where you are, where you've been, the direction is up with wings like eagles! Isaiah 40:31 – "But those who hope in the Lord will renew their strength. They will soar on wings like eagles; they will run and not grow weary, they will walk and not be faint."

Tina D. Lewis is a 3-Time International Best-Selling Author, Philanthropist, blazing Sales, and Marketing Expert, the CEO of Royalty Coaching LLC, and the Catalyst of The 6-Figure Incubator, a multi-functional powerhouse execution firm, known for producing six-figure businesses for women from around the globe, built for exponential success.

Affectionately known as the "Bottom Line" Queen, Tina specializes in creating tangible wealth opportunities in the lives of both vetted and budding professionals, helping them eliminate minuscule thinking, stagnant business reflexes, and one-dimensional branding. She has helped many entrepreneurs; including an exclusive women's branch from her non-profit organization: Her Business Matters to overcome the delusion of underperformance, to shift their mindset, and gain the clarity necessary to transform their businesses forever. Her Mantra is simple: After it is all said and done, the most important question is... "What's your Bottom Line?" - Tina D. Lewis. Revenue Generator. Executor. Mogul.

Facebook & Instagram: @tinadlewis
Clubhouse @tinadlewis
Website: www.tinadlewis.com

18

Navigating Through Life

"ONE MOMENT AT A TIME. One moment at a time." It's what I would continue to embrace as we began to navigate through what many of us would call a global pandemic, but I would like to consider it as being, uncharted territory. In my few years of living, I have experienced some pretty interesting things, but I wouldn't say that I have witnessed a series of events that indeed impacted the way that the entire world would be able to function.

Of course, I've heard of smallpox, tuberculosis, and the most fatal pandemic recorded, the plague. But never would I have ever imagined experiencing a global pandemic in my lifetime. But anything is possible, right? Grief, Uncertainty, and Loss for many, was a song that remained on repeat for so many different families throughout the world. Every news station or social media outlet were constantly reporting updates of people losing their lives due to this horrible virus. For many, this entire experience has been the opportunity to have a new outlook on life. And for others, there has been lots of heartbreak and uncertainty.

Cancelled.

Webster's definition says, "to order (something already arranged, such as a meeting or event) to be postponed indefinitely; call off." This was the theme that rang true for so many across the world. This experience was by far the most foreign experience that I had yet to experience. I know myself well enough to know that oftentimes, when it comes to change, I can become a bit apprehensive, and at that point, anxiety tries to creep in. I guess you can sum it up to the fear of not knowing what things would look like from this point forward. However, this was the perfect opportunity for me to trust in God who is truly so faithful. And an opportunity to discover ways to help keep the anxiety to a minimum. A few things that have helped me and still does are working out; movement helps a lot, journaling my thoughts, painting, reading, and listening to music. At this point, working from home for months was my new normal and that has been a true blessing within itself. Unfortunately, during this pandemic, there were thousands of individuals that were without work. In this, it has been so evident that God has still provided. This may have looked very different for everyone, but I am hopeful that many have come to trust Him more.

One sure thing that I can say about navigating through this very uncertain time, Holy Spirit has been so strategic as it relates to guidance and provision. I would say that this time has been a very vulnerable time for me as well. And out of this place, God has given me the courage and grace needed to share a part of my testimony through writing. Healing is what resulted from this exchange and peace has led the way. I know that the scripture tells us that, "Where the spirit of the Lord is there is liberty." Freedom. That's what I began to walk in. For many years of my life, I had begun to believe the lies of the enemy, like God is not pleased with me and I am my past decisions. But I begin to renew my mind with what is true. And the Holy Spirit has reminded me that I am free. I am His. I am loved. I am chosen. I am the righteousness of Christ. Thank you, JESUS. I won't begin to boast on how during this time God has opened doors that only He could. But what I will tell you is, He is doing a new thing in me. His hand has been so evident throughout it all. The slowing down of the everyday routine is a blessing that I will forever cherish. This has given so many the opportunity to rest. Rest is holy, I truly believe that. Rest, reset, refocus, and recharge, is exactly what many did. And I dare not leave out that for many, grieving, pain, and hurt have become a part of our journeys as well.

Isaiah 41:10 reminds us of why we should not fear. God is with us, and He will strengthen us. This is one scripture that I must continue to cling to as I navigate through life's challenges. If you are reading this, I would like to encourage you with this. Regardless of what your situation may look like, please remember that we have a Father in heaven that loves us unconditionally, and He has a great future for us all, regardless of what may be currently surrounding us. Jeremiah 29:11 reminds us of this very thing. Remember His promises, they always come to pass. "God is not like man that He should lie." Our feelings and our understanding may fail us, but God will not. That's why scripture reminds us that we should "Trust in The Lord, with All of our heart and lean not to our own understanding..." there is a freedom in trusting.

It is my prayer that God's peace keeps you as you continue to navigate through your life's journey. Remember to abide in Him and He has promised that He would do the same. And if you do not have a relationship with Jesus Christ and you would like Him to come into your heart, Romans 10:9 tells us, "That if you confess with your mouth Jesus as Lord and believe in your heart that Christ raised Him from the dead, you shall be saved." It's truly that simple. Until later, I love you, but God is madly in love with you. Your sister in Christ, Miracle.

Miracle Turner Peters was born and raised in Covington, La. Miracle is a best-selling author of Dear Single Mom: You Were Built to Defy the Odds, a Motivational Speaker, and mother of one amazing son. Miracle is the CEO/Owner of Rooted in Love, LLC. Rooted in Love is a community that believes in spreading love and encouragement. Whether it is through writing or providing inspiring apparel, we will get it done. Her passions include traveling to new places, exploring new dishes, and encouraging others.

If you would like to contact me:
Contact info:
Email: rootedinlove21@gmail.com
Website: http://rootedinloveshop.com/
Facebook: www.facebook.com/miracle.lyna.7
Instagram: https://www.instagram.com/__rooted_in_love/

19

Trust the Process

I DIDN'T KNOW WHAT TO expect from this pandemic because the whole world literally shut down. My job shut down and sent me home on March 15, 2020. I am thankful that I continued to get paid throughout the pandemic because I worked at home. I liked working from home in the beginning, but it soon became very tiring. I really missed being around people and going out with my friends. I immediately realized that things were not going back to normal any time soon.

What I have gained from this pandemic is a closeness to God and emotional healing. Being alone forced me to take a long hard look at myself and question how I could improve to make an impact in my life and the life of others. I began sitting quietly before God and listening for His voice. I wrote down in a journal what I heard His Spirit say to me. God is always speaking. God told me that He is going to resurrect the things that He allowed to die in my life. I had to die so God could birth something new in my life. The promises that He made to me are still yes and amen. Sometimes we can receive a promise from God, but the timing is wrong. In other words, I was not emotionally prepared to start a ministry, and it did not flourish the way that I thought it should. I realized that I did not give the ministry the attention that it required because I was not completely healed within myself. A planted flower requires water, nutrients, and attention in order to flourish. I planted the ministry too soon. I needed inner healing from emotional wounds from my past.

Being home 24/7, during this pandemic, provided an opportunity for me to receive counseling and do the hard work of facing the ugly truth about my past hurt. I realized that I was bitter and wallowing in my pain, which was hindering my blessings from coming forth. I was committing self-sabotage and I was also sabotaging relationships. I was always the person that everyone came to when he/she needed to talk. I was often told that I'm very easy to talk to and they don't know why they are telling me their business. God gave me the gift of counseling before I ever knew that I had it. I have always loved small groups and discussions of issues and solutions. God was preparing me at a young age.

What I was not prepared for were the hard knocks and disappointments of life. I had unrealistic expectations of how life and love should be. When it did not go as I had planned in my mind, I shut down and became bitter instead of better. I felt betrayed, rejected, and unloved. I saw the world through hurt and rejected eyes.

Being at home for well over a year, provided the opportunity to get the proper help and healing that I so desperately needed to heal, grow, and move past this dark place of loneliness, rejection, and hurt. Now that I've done the work and healed, God has released me to re-launch my ministry that I started years ago. Timing is everything! This period of self-reflection and healing has allowed me plenty of time to receive God's love. As a result, I have nurtured and watered past and present relationships. God showed me that people need each other to survive. God never intended for man to be alone. I have been more intentional about cultivating relationships. I see things from a different perspective now. I see through the lens of love instead of rejection.

I am grateful, thankful, and blessed to have spent this time alone so that God can really deal with me on a deep level. It's important to slow down and get quiet before God so that He can reveal things to you. God desires true intimacy with us as well. It is not always pretty, but it is worth taking heed to get free from emotional and spiritual baggage. This pandemic has brought me closer to family and friends. It made me realize that all the material things don't mean anything. We can't take any of that with us when we leave this earth. Relationships need to be restored, watered, and nurtured. We need to serve God in the capacity that He has given us to serve.

Life is precious and we should treat it as such. We should win souls and glorify God in everything that we do. Our life is a gift to God. Get healed so that you can use your gifts and talents to minister to others and win lost souls to Christ. There is always a light at the end of a tunnel. My light was the fact that I got healed and delivered from emotional baggage that I didn't know I was carrying around. I have unpacked and dropped off my emotional baggage. Thank You, Jesus!

Even when it does not look like you think it should, trust the process. Jesus died for our sins because He trusted the process. God has a purpose and a plan for each of our lives, but we must trust the process. Pruning never feels good but the process is where the old comes off to make room for the new. Olives are crushed during the process and the oil (anointing) is revealed. Grapes are crushed during the process to produce the new wine (anointing). Pruning and crushing are part of the process. Trust the process.

"Blessed is the man who trusts in the Lord, and whose hope is the Lord. For he shall be like a tree planted by the waters, which spreads out its roots by the river, and will not fear when heat comes; but its leaf will be green, and will not be anxious in the year of drought, nor will cease from yielding fruit." Jeremiah 17:7-8

Evangelane Turner is a four-time Best Selling Author, Certified Professional Life Coach, a Christian Counselor, and a licensed minister. She holds a Bachelor of Arts in Social Services, along with a Master of Science in Leadership. She has a passion and a heart for others. Evangelane has led several support groups in areas such as marital healing, grief recovery, and family restoration. Being a mentor in the singles ministry has allowed her to unleash her fun side. Evangelane is a proud mother of a son and a grandmother of two little girls. Evangelane currently resides in Memphis, Tennessee.

Facebook: Evangelane Turner
Email: Evangelane.Turner@gmail.com

20

Positioned for the Pour

2020 WAS A YEAR LIKE NO OTHER, it was my Golden Year; the year of my 30th birthday! My friends, family, and I made plans to go to Turk's & Caicos in February to celebrate my golden year. Historically, I imagined myself spending my 30th birthday with my husband, or at the very least, my husband-to-be, but I was still...as single as a dollar bill. To be honest, it bothered me more than I was ever willing to openly admit. I was always the one invited to weddings, asked to be a bridesmaid, attending baby showers and anniversary celebrations; plus being the one consistently typing "CONGRATULATIONS" under anyone's post that read "I Said Yes." Nonetheless, I was thrilled to spend my Golden Year with my family and friends. I covered the resort expenses for everyone and flights for my immediate family members; God blessed me more than I could ever ask for with a great 8 months in my brand-new career as a real estate broker.

As I was preparing to order my outfits for the trip, I heard on the news about a virus called COVID-19 that was slowly creeping through the nation, but it wasn't present in the United States nor was it present in Turk's & Caicos; therefore, I wasn't too worried about the virus. I arrived in Turks & Caicos on February 18, 2020, with my mom, aunt, cousin, sisters, and my good friend Mich'e—who was actually a client at the time, in the process of building her family's new construction home—we met for the very first time at the resort. By day 4, I was completely over-paying $20 for a hamburger and a water, plus looking at water all day, every day. When we arrived back in the United States, it was very different at the airport; we needed to wear face masks, sanitize our hands, complete additional paperwork and stand in long lines depending on where we traveled from.

Once we arrived in North Carolina, I was ready to get back to work in my new career as a real estate broker, when suddenly, we were placed on a statewide lockdown. The COVID-19 virus that I was initially not concerned about was beginning to spread rapidly, and people were being hospitalized due to the side effects. Fear slowly but surely began to creep in. For starters, I did not have health insurance; therefore, if I was found positive, would I survive? Secondly, I was in a sales-based career; therefore, if I can't work, I can't make money. I remember my dad texting me to assure me that regardless of what happens in the real estate market, he has my back regarding my wellbeing and finances. I prayed to God, vividly saying, "Lord, don't let my faith fail." Truth be told, the future didn't look promising, everything was uncertain at this point; life as we once knew it was completely turned upside down. The news informed us that citizens were dying at an alarming rate, jobs were forcing employees to work from home, hundreds of thousands of people were laid off, we fought over toilet tissue and can foods at the grocery store, we avoided being near anyone, even those we knew and loved. And all the while I kept praying, "Lord, don't let my faith fail."

During the lockdown, I watched everything, I ate everything, I prayed more, I wrote my first book and sent it to a publishing company. I attempted to lose weight, develop new habits, break old habits, and try to still remain in business. Also, I reflected heavily on the promises of God; I always write down things that are prophesied over my life so that I can give God praise when it comes to pass. In 2018, Pastor Shyremia Latham told me my husband will be high ranking in the military and I'd meet him in Fayetteville, NC. Finally, the lockdown was lifted, and I received an inbox on Instagram from a guy named Aaron, he was an officer in the Army looking to purchase a home because he was PCSing here to Fayetteville, NC. After searching for a couple of weeks, we found the home he wanted, which was a 5-bedroom, 3-bathroom, 3 car garage new construction home;

our closing date was September 1st. On August 11th, another prophet told me that in 3 months, God was going to birth a very beautiful relationship out of nowhere. On November 11th, Aaron asked me to be his girlfriend by presenting me with a pink perfectly wrapped box that contained a pink house he made and painted with a "SOLD" sign on the door and a picture of him. My eyes were filled with tears.

I closed out 2020 with a heart of gratitude, I sold 42 homes in the midst of a global pandemic, I became #7 in the state of North Carolina amongst ROG agents for sales, I was #1 Producer of the Year, I met the love of my life, who I later discovered checked off everything I asked for when I wrote a letter to God in May 2019; Aaron moved back to Fayetteville, NC in May 2020.

Oftentimes, we focus on what surrounds us, and we forget that God is still in control. God is surrounding whatever is surrounding you! I pray over every reader that even in the midst of adversity, uncertainty, and confusion, every promise, desire, and plan from our Father will prevail. In Jesus's Name, Amen.

"For I know the plans I have for you, declares the Lord, plans to prosper you and not to harm you. Plans to give you hope and a future." – Jeremiah 29:11

Kendra L Conyers is an advocate for empowering women and an inspirational trailblazer of this generation. She is a native of Fayetteville, North Carolina. She holds a bachelor's degree in psychology and a master's degree in marriage counseling. Kendra is a North Carolina Luxury Real Estate Broker and a Real Estate Investor. Due to her personality, expertise, and drive, Kendra has quickly become a sought out real estate professional. She was voted Top 5 Best Realtors in 2019 and made Top 100 North Carolina Realtors on social media in 2020. In November 2020, Kendra was #3 in the state for sales amongst ROG agents. Kendra is also the founder of Girls of Grace Foundation, Inc., which is a nonprofit organization where she mentors at-risk teens in her community.

www.kendraconyers.com
IG @kendralconyers IG @girlsofgraceinc

21

Pandemic and My Passion

WHEN I MEET NEW PEOPLE that know nothing about me, the first two questions they ask are, "What's your name and where are you from?" Then comes the ultimate brutal judgmental question, "What do you do?" This took some time, but now I absolutely enjoy and find it hilarious when I see people's reaction after I tell them. It's like they are 10 out of 10 shocked when I tell them I'm a full-time Artistic Dog Groomer. Most people have this constipated look on their face as they're trying to remain serious and nod, but deep down, they want to burst out laughing and say, "What, you're a what?!"

Most people actually do laugh in my face, and I'm eagerly waiting to laugh with them. Like in all seriousness; I'm like, right it's so hilarious, trust me! I didn't see it coming either, and if someone told me one year ago that this is what

I'd be doing, I'd think they were absolutely crazy. And now actually, my business is doing extremely well and shockingly took off very rapidly. Now, I can honestly and proudly say that there isn't anything else I'd rather be doing or be. Just six months ago, I never could see myself proudly laughing with strangers, I was actually terrified of being laughed at and purposely not wanting to tell people what I was planning to do because I didn't want to be judged or be made fun of because it wasn't the coolest thing, the most popular or the highest paying job.

I've always been known for having this top-dollar luxury life and "Dog Groomer Income" is nowhere in that category. But the word judged has been completely turned, I feel, and know now, I'm inspiring others to be like me, so what if it is not popular, follow your heart and purpose regardless of anything! If your absolutely 100 percent true about it, it WILL pay off. This may sound ironic, but Covid was the reason for this passion reveal. I'm honestly still in shock to this day on how this all played out so smoothly. I have 2 Maltese that I have had for 8 years; I have faithfully always taken them to the groomer regularly. Grooming them myself had never, ever crossed my mind until Covid hit. I just couldn't stand the sight of my poor fur babes looking like abused mops, which meant that something had to be done. So, I boldly ordered a starter dog groomer clipper off Amazon and said what the heck. I was their only hope at this point since the groomers were closed and who knew for how long. Mind you, I did do hair as a side hustle back in my high school and college days so it was a chance they wouldn't turn out "that bad."

At the time when I received the starter groomer kit, I was working full-time at my previous job, CBD wholesale products, and during that time, we were selling wholesale hand sanitizer. That time when hand sanitizers couldn't be found anywhere, and we happened to have it in 55-gallon drums in massive supply. My phone was off the ringer until 3 am and back at 7 am. It was massive crazy dollar deals, but it was honestly the most intense time in my career. I felt like the hand sanitizer was like crack and everyone was desperate to get it to put it on their shelves.

So back to the dog grooming, there I was, taking a break from the crazy demanding people, sitting on my hard wood floor with these poor Maltese mops on my vanity stool as a groomer table, and I just went for it. I didn't watch YouTube tutorial; I just knew how I wanted them to look and decided to cut away until they looked relatively close to the vision I had. I was using super sharp scissors and clippers, and it was late at night and the vet was close in case I accidentally nicked them, so I was forced to take my sweet time and be extremely careful as possible. My fur babies were confused as heck as to what I was about to attempt to do. Four hours later, I shockingly did the most therapeutic thing ever. After months of doing intense nonstop work, I was finally doing something that forced me to slow down for once and take my precious time and just mentally getting away from this world's pure craziness. It felt so good to my soul, and the dogs looked great, considering it was my first time. And just like that, I literally said, "I could actually make a career outta this," I enjoyed every second of it, and immediately enrolled in an all-breed groomer course.

I picked it up just like that, but it really wasn't as simple as it sounds. This passion reveal was a perfect combo of what I had already been passionate about my whole life. Most people don't know that I went to Pre-vet school twice and dropped out both times. Why, because my heart was there a million times over for the animals, but my interest in Biology and Medical Terminology was a struggle due to super lack of interest. A funny fact that most people also don't know is that my mother told me how as a very young toddler, I could make every animal sound perfectly before I could even say a complete sentence. I was a girl that grew up in the country, and my mother and grandmother were always gifting me with endless pets because of my love and connection for them.

So, handling dogs and animals alone has always been second nature to me. I learned from an early age to study their body language, which is how they do 80% of their communication. So, when veterinary school didn't work, I leaned towards my passion in the glam industry that consists of photography, modeling, and doing hair and makeup. I was self-taught in the hair industry, creating looks as a side hustle in high school and college. I was able to create almost any style on my own hair after just seeing it. I just had this "eye" for creating. Glam is just something I see as true art, like a blank canvas with space to create something that could hold my signature alone.

A quick story on how I met Alandria Lloyd, the one who orchestrated this entire book project. The one who has also been my mentor since day one, almost a year ago. She is the one who helped to connect the dots of how to use the tools I already had. So, to back it up just a little; I gave my life back to Christ three years ago in the midst of relocating my entire life and environment. In order for me to live fully into whatever God had for me, I needed to literally pack everything and just leave everything I was once comfortable with. Once I took that bold risk with a huge leap of faith, I became completely drowned in His presence. It became more of a need to feel whole and literally all I cared about. I was desperate to truly know Him. Because how can you have a relationship with anyone and communicate if you don't know them?

I was literally all in because I had already lived the life Whitney wanted and I failed myself over and over. I was in a complete surrender state and allowing God to have His way because nothing else was working. So, in these church events, where I spent so much of my time because I truly felt it was a safe place, there was a fire. The saying, "church hurt," I experienced it first-hand, and it was literally a huge emotional set-back for my healing. But now after time, God revealed that it was something that needed to be done because I was having unrealistic expectations of people with "titles," when in reality everyone on this earth is just as human as I am. Also, in the midst of this hurt, it put me in a position to allow myself to meet people that needed to be in my circle to help with my next step in my journey, and one of those key people was Alandria.

I have only been a pro groomer for six months, but this process started three years ago. Three years full of healing, starting with extreme detox, acceptance of what was, and surrendering to be filled with what God truly had for me. I wish I could say it was easy; but I'd honestly do it over again in a heartbeat due to the reward that came with it. I had to deal with isolation before Covid even was a topic, I had to let go of all my comfort areas, I had to readapt to unknown territory. But God has molded and given me remarkable wisdom and strength in it all. I am truly the happiest I've ever been. I've never been so sure of everything around me and so sure of who I am now as a person. So don't be afraid to surrender and to obey the tug of God's orders, for His plans for us are truly greater than we can ever imagine.

Whitney Mitchell would like to step in and stand up for the ones that have those "unpopular passions and dreams" or the road less traveled where the blueprint is limited and nearly bare. That solid blueprint that is needed, you know deep down, can only be given and supplied by God. Whitney Mitchell is a full-time Artistic Dog Groomer that launched her first business mid-Covid. When she tells people this, they remind her of how they expected her to be a Real Estate Agent or Fashion Model based on her track record.

Before pursuing her passion, she had an opportunity to learn first-hand what it means when people say, "Some people are so broke that all they have is money." Whitney had everything in hand but still had a deep emptiness, and she was desperate for more. Whitney had tried everything possible, leaving the last option for help, her faith. Whitney's faith is what miraculously saved her; it literally gave her a second wind and showed her the passions and purpose that were always there were more powerful than she could ever imagine.

22

The Promise Land

EARLY ONE SUNDAY MORNING, I woke up to the sun shining through my window. As I lay there watching the sun peer inside my bedroom, I thought to myself, "Today will be a good day." As I began getting ready for church, I began listening to praise and worship. While I was busy making sure that every hair was in place, the song "What About the Children" by Yolanda Adams came on. This song serves as a reminder for me that "Weeping may endure for a night, but joy comes in the morning" Psalm 30:5. I was in my mother's den crying out to God after yet another failed suicide attempt, the first time I ever heard this song.

When I heard the song, I thought about just how far I had come. How my joy had come and the fact that I was now completely healed and whole from sexual trauma from my childhood. That night as I slept, I had a dream that I was being fired from my job. I vividly saw them sitting me down and firing me. I had no clue as to why I would be fired from my job. It was not until I got the call that the nonprofit organization that I had been working for was laying us off. Once again, I heard "Joy comes in the morning." God said it was time for me to write my first book. Since I was a young girl, I always wanted to write a book but never knew what to really write about. God spoke and told me, "Unspoken Truth: The Aftermath of Sexual Abuse," it would be about my own personal testimony of sexual trauma. So as 2019 ended, I was made to sit still and work on just my book alone. Not one day did He allow anything to be disconnected nor did I stress about anything financially at all.

While I was gearing up for what I thought would have been the best year of my life, the pandemic hit in March of 2020. My book was released on April 1, 2020. The success of the book was phenomenal in more ways than one. The book prompted me to start helping others that had experienced sexual trauma. From there, I started my own nonprofit organization entitled S.W.A.G, which stands for Sexual Wellness Advocacy Group. The mission is to support survivors in their healing by way of educating and transforming society's response to sexual trauma.

My book and the start of my new business adventure was perfect timing. There were a lot of people that struggled during the quarantine due to being in the house alone with the thoughts of their own trauma. God spoke yet again and said, "I tell you the truth, when you did it to one of the least of these my brothers and sisters you were doing it to me" Matthew 25:40. I knew then that God had brought me through to bring someone else through. So, from there, I began to get the S.W.A.G name out there via social media. Once a day, if not several times a day, S.W.A.G. would be interviewing or being interviewed by other organizations by way of Facebook or Instagram. I would take calls all hours of the day and night and people were loving the fact that I was offering services during the pandemic. It was a privilege and an honor to be doing what God called me to do. However, just twenty-two days after my book came out, one of my cousins lost her life due to complications of the Covid-19 virus at the age of 29. At her funeral, I watched as those doves flew high in her memory; it broke my heart to pieces. I could not help but think about all the times that I tried to commit suicide, and one virus came in and took out a slew of folks for no reason at all. I decided to use her death as an empowering tool for me to keep moving forward, helping others to heal.

In July, I was invited as a speaker for the "Coastal Fashion Week." Initially, when I spoke with the young lady and she invited me to speak in Dallas, Texas, I was excited and immediately said yes. However, the day before the event, my husband and I made the trip to Texas, that night is when reality set in that I would be speaking about sexual trauma at a fashion show. The day of the event, I was so nervous. I felt as though I should have turned around and gone back home. I just knew that people would be looking at me all crazy because they were there to see a fashion show, right? It was totally the opposite of what I thought. After I had spoken, I had just a few minutes left over, and I opened the floor up for questions. The hands that flew up from men and women alike was amazing. They absolutely loved everything that I had to offer at the event.

Afterwards, there was so many people that stopped by my table afterwards, weather to buy a book or just to say thanks for telling my story. I knew that night that I was truly in the land that God had promised me. This was the Joy that cometh in the morning. Years ago, I would have never imagined being completely healed and made whole from sexual trauma. I would have never thought that I could forgive my uncle for what he had done to me.

It took me twenty-eight long years to be healed and whole. I know personally, forgiveness was my biggest hold up in my deliverance. Once I chose to forgive those that had wronged me, then windows from heaven opened for me. I made it to the promised land! I now help others to go to the promised land, the land of freedom.

Alisha White is a Life Coach, a sexual trauma advocate, and a deaconess. In 2020, she became the bestselling author of "Unspoken Truth: The Aftermath of Sexual Abuse."

Mrs. White is the Founder/Executive Director of S.W.A.G. which stands for "Sexual Wellness Advocacy Group." The 501c3 nonprofit organization was founded to help others to heal from sexual trauma. Mrs. white wants victims to know that they are not alone in this process. She also supports families in keeping their loved ones from becoming a victim and what to do if it should happen to you. She encourages people of all ages, ethnicity, and gender to use their voices to make the world a better place.

Alisha White is the epitome of what life looks like on the other side of sexual trauma. Her mission in life is to help others to heal from sexual trauma one person at a time.

www.swagbr.org
swagbr911@gmail.com
Facebook: Alisha Newbins white
Instagram: s.w.a.g._br

23

The Year of Reconstruction

NO MATTER WHO YOU TALK TO about the coronavirus pandemic, you will hear some type of story of tragedies, job losses, economic hardships, financial struggles, and loss of loved ones. On the other side of that, many people have stories about opening new businesses, growth, victories in their personal lives, families becoming closer, and restored relationships.

See, I believe it's all about your focus (i.e., are you thinking about the positive or negative) of your situation. What desire is in your heart? What are you believing God for? I like to look at the pandemic as a reconstruction period because God had to rebuild some things that were damaged and destroyed. I would like to take you back through the year, starting with January 2020. For most people, the beginning of the year is about planning, goal setting, and implementation. We all know the saying, "2020 is gonna be my best year!" So, my husband and I set goals for our family, marriage, personal, spiritual, finances, and our business. When I tell you, we went ALL out and dreamed big for the year, we went ALL OUT!

We were excited and extremely optimistic that it would be our best year in life and business. We were praying, doing affirmations, and working hard daily for the thing we were believing God to do for and through us. We had already begun to see things changing for the better! Who knew God had other plans? I remember Friday, March 13th, 2020; it was announced that schools were closing. Everything after that seemed like a blur because I knew something was happening that I'd only read about in the past. We were watching and listening to too much news, and I started to worry! Off to the grocery store I went to stock up and prepare for the worst because everyone was talking about the country shutting down. The stores were crazy and chaotic! I remember calling my mother, who was in another store, and we were trying to help each other find the supplies we needed. Empty shelves were EVERYWHERE!

Fear started to settle in because of the chaos and unknown, and my mind started wondering. I started to think about all the plans we made for my "best year." And all of the things that I wanted to accomplish were conducive to us doing well in our business and growing as a person. There were some changes that I wanted to make. I also started to think, "Oh my God! Will my own business even survive a crisis like this? And how long will we have to be shut down?" I tried to shift my thinking by praying and meditating, and I remember saying, "God, I know your promises are sure. And you have never failed us!" That changed my perspective on what was happening around me. I told my husband no more news and to "TURN IT OFF!" I started saying, "We operate in God's economy," and those were the words I needed to move forward. Our entire life as I knew it changed seemingly overnight for the better. I want to share areas that I was impacted the most (family/marriage, personally, business).

Everything was closed and there was nowhere to go. This allowed me to spend countless hours with my family. We were looking for ways to stay occupied, so we had talks that we were normally too busy to have. Being stuck inside with our kids really allowed us to grow a closer bond. When I looked back at my goals, I had written down one thing, and that was to do more family activities and spend more time together. I feel like God granted my wish. In our yearly goal-setting session, I realized that if I was going to achieve the things I had written. I had to evolve and become a better version of me. I believe all success starts within. God places everything in you to fulfill His purpose, but it's how you think, feel, and see yourself. I prayed for personal and spiritual growth. It was funny to me, how God allowed the world to stop so I could learn more about myself. I had plenty of time to think, reflect, self-evaluate, and meditate. My talks with God became more frequent, but I listened more also. This time allowed me to grow closer to him and changed my perspective in the way I see life situations.

As far as our business goes, God exceeded our expectations. We experienced massive growth and expansion to multiple states. Our income doubled working from home! Not only did He show up mightily for the things we were praying for, but other people in business with us had a record-breaking year also. We promoted our first regional VP business partner. God enlarged our territory just as we had been praying The Prayer of Jabez. Earlier, I said our goals were conducive to our business doing well, and though it did, that's not where my trust was. Believing and trusting God allowed Him to work in my life in ways I never imagined he would! Especially in a time when the world was in a "state of emergency." The pandemic changed many lives and totally changed mine as well. All I know is......God kept his promises.

Jeremiah 29: 11-14 NLT; *"For I know the plans I have for you" says the Lord. "They are plans for good and not for disaster, to give you a future and a hope. In those days when you pray, I will listen. If you look for me wholeheartedly, you will find me. I will be found by you," says the Lord. "I will end your captivity and restore your fortunes. I will gather you out of the nations where I sent you and will bring you home again to your own land."*

Toya Glover is a loving wife to Daniel Glover for 18 years and a mother of three wonderful children. She resides in Independence, La. And was born and raised in Hammond, La. She is the oldest sibling of three children. She is a best-selling author, financial coach, and mentor. She along with her husband run their own financial service agency where they educate and empower families economically by teaching them how to build and obtain wealth.

Toya loves Christ, being an entrepreneur, her family, and traveling the world. She also loves reading and journaling about her life experiences and even writes prayers to God. She always had the desire to write a book to help other women by sharing her story of being a teenage mother and vowed that she would break the generational curse of teen pregnancy with her son. Her life's desire is to inspire women to believe that your life does not have to stop at your mistakes.

24

Prosperity During Famine

THE "GREAT" PANDEMIC OF 2020 will forever be echoed and etched in history. Sometimes I still have a hard time believing that it happened during our lifetime. When I first heard about the Corona Virus, I really didn't take it seriously. On March 13, 2020, I was boarding a plane, heading to Indiana for a preaching assignment. Everyone was trying to project their fears onto me by telling me that I shouldn't go, but I went anyway. I felt that God would protect me, and He did just that. When I returned, I still didn't take it seriously because I just knew God would provide. However, I had a vision, and I saw people standing in line waiting to get into grocery stores where they were only allowing three people in at a time. After the vision, I heard the Holy Spirit say, "Go to the store and purchase enough goods to last at least two weeks."

I immediately headed to the store to stock up. At that moment, I realized that things were changing and that they would never quite be the same. As an entrepreneur, I didn't know what would happen, BUT I knew God was going to take care of us. You see, the pandemic may have been a global crisis, but I've had several personal crises, so I was no stranger to tight or tough times. I went into my prayer closet and began to decree and declare what I wanted to see in the midst of the pandemic. I spoke things such as, "I will prosper during this pandemic." "I will make more money during this global crisis." "God, I trust you to enlarge my territory and propel me during the pandemic."

The news reporters were constantly reporting negativity, such as the daily death rate, the increase of hospital admissions, and the number of businesses that were shutting down. Their level of consistency encouraged me to consistently speak the good news and shine light in the areas of darkness. Life and death are truly in the power of the tongue, and I witnessed it manifest in my life like never before! The more I declared prosperity, the more it manifested before my very eyes. I was blessed to triple my income in 2020. I served more clients and helped hundreds create their own businesses. I released two books during the pandemic and taught countless aspiring authors how to share their testimonies in published books. My clients were also able to double and even triple their income, and many left their jobs and became full-time entrepreneurs.

So many great things have happened, but what's really amazing is how God truly manifested His power. During a time when everyone expected total decline, God used that moment to increase and prosper His people. Jehovah Jireh provided in ways people never expected. Jehovah Shammah was there to comfort and wrap His loving arms around His children. Jehovah Rapha healed many who were afflicted from COVID-19. Jehovah Gibbor fought for us in ways we will never fully understand. Yahweh was truly a present help for us during times of trouble. Many who were following New Age trends have now developed a genuine relationship with the Father, and I give Him glory for it all.

During the pandemic, my son began his senior year in high school. I didn't want him to return to school, so he became a virtual student. He graduated from high school with honors (Magna Cum Laude) and will soon start his own business during this pandemic. My family is alive and well, and we praise God for keeping us.

I have mentioned a lot of great milestones, however, I cannot forget one that I hold near to my heart, and that is the discovery of self. I have learned so much about myself as a woman, mother, leader, entrepreneur, and a woman of God. I have learned how to obey the first time. You see, God speaks to all of us, but many times, we choose to ignore His voice and do things our way. In the height of the pandemic, God instructed me to move. He told me to pack up everything that would fit in my small car and move to another state. Once again, there were those who tried to project their fears onto me, but I was determined to obey His voice even when I could not see the way.

Before I made a move, I went back to the prayer closet. You see, the prayer closet is the place for strategy. After I prayed, God led me to the area where I was supposed to move. I applied for the place and was instantly approved. So many people sowed into me and gave me money for the move. Everything fell into place, and it was the easiest move I have ever had. Once I moved, I was led to open an office for my publishing company. I was hesitant, but I obeyed. My obedience was the key that opened the door to prosperity. God's mighty hand destroyed barriers that tried to come against me. Since I've moved, my influence, impact, and income have quadrupled. I just want to encourage you to move at the sound of His voice. No matter how uncomfortable it may be, just do it. Do it in faith, knowing that God is with you, His hand is on you, His favor has gone before you, His grace covers you, and His presence surrounds you. Therefore, you have no excuse! The pandemic has proven that God is faithful, and though, the pandemic has been great, God is greater!

Alandria Lloyd is a known as the "The Author's Advocate" who teaches aspiring and published authors how to use their words as keys to unlock unlimited opportunities. She shows aspiring authors how to complete their nonfiction books within 24-hours. Alandria also coaches published authors by teaching them how to turn their books in a sustainable business.

She is also a serial entrepreneur, award-winning, 15X bestselling author, and award-winning philanthropist. Alandria is the owner of a book publishing company, The Writer's Block LLC. The Writer's Block offers coaching, consultations, and premium book publishing options. Her company also offers memberships to teach others how to build 6-figure publishing companies.

To contact Alandria, you can send an email to info@thewritersblockllc.com or visit bit.ly/TWBclarity to schedule a free call.

The authors of "Kept Promises" would like to thank you for your support! If you enjoyed this book, please do us a favor and leave a 5-star review on Amazon.

If you are an aspiring author who would like to be a part of the next anthology, or if you would like to work on a solo project. Please contact The Writer's Block LLC by sending an email to info@thewritersblockllc.com. You can also visit bit.ly/TWBclarity to schedule a free 15-minute call to discuss your vision.

www.ingramcontent.com/pod-product-compliance
Lightning Source LLC
Chambersburg PA
CBHW070043100426
42740CB00013B/2779